The AuDHD Advantage

Transform Your Neurodivergent Traits into
Real-World Success

Ludwig Steven Cox

This book contains information and strategies based on the author's research, personal experiences, and observations within the neurodivergent community. It is not intended as a substitute for professional medical advice, diagnosis, or treatment. Always seek the advice of qualified health providers with questions you may have regarding any medical or psychological condition.

The strategies and suggestions presented may not be suitable for every individual. Results will vary based on individual circumstances, neurotype expression, co-occurring conditions, and implementation of the concepts presented.

All names and identifying details of individuals mentioned in case studies and examples throughout this book have been changed to protect privacy. Any resemblance to actual persons, living or deceased, or actual events is purely coincidental. Some examples represent composite experiences drawn from multiple sources within the neurodivergent community.

The author and publisher disclaim any liability arising directly or indirectly from the use of this book.

Table of Contents

Chapter 1: More Than a Disorder

You've probably heard it all before. The struggles, the challenges, the "deficits." Every article, every assessment, every well-meaning professional starts with what's supposedly wrong with your brain. But here's what they're missing - and it's huge. Your AuDHD brain isn't broken. It's running different software, and that software has capabilities most people can't even access.

Think about it this way. You wouldn't judge a Swiss Army knife by how well it hammers nails, right? You'd look at all those different tools and think about the unique problems it can solve. Your brain works the same way. It's got tools and functions that others don't have, and once you understand what they are and how to use them, everything changes.

The Convergence Zone: Where Autism Meets ADHD

For the longest time, professionals thought autism and ADHD were completely separate things. Like oil and water. They'd tell parents, "Your child can't have both." Boy, were they wrong. Turns out, these two neurotypes don't just coexist - they create something entirely new when they come together.

When autism meets ADHD in your brain, you get this fascinating convergence zone. It's not just autism plus ADHD, like adding two numbers together. It's more like mixing yellow and blue to get green - you end up with something that has its own unique properties.

Your autistic side brings incredible pattern recognition, deep systematic thinking, and the ability to spot tiny details others miss. It's the part of you that notices when something's out of place, that can't let go of inconsistencies, that builds beautiful mental models of how things work. This is the part that gives you that laser focus when something truly interests you.

Meanwhile, your ADHD side brings rapid-fire connections, creative leaps, and the ability to see possibilities everywhere. It's the part that gets excited about seventeen different projects, that makes unexpected connections between totally unrelated ideas, that keeps your mind buzzing with "what if" scenarios.

Now here's where it gets interesting. Most people think these two sides would fight each other. And sure, sometimes they do. But more often, they're dancing together in ways that create pure magic. Your ADHD generates ideas at lightning speed, and your autism analyzes them with surgical precision. Your autism creates detailed mental maps, and your ADHD finds shortcuts and novel paths through them.

Sarah, a 32-year-old game developer, describes it perfectly: "My ADHD brain is like a idea factory running 24/7, churning out concepts and connections. My autistic brain is quality control, taking those ideas and stress-testing them against every pattern and system I know. Together, they help me create game mechanics that are both wildly creative and mathematically elegant."

Breaking Down the Deficit Model: Why Traditional Narratives Limit Potential

The deficit model. Even the name makes you feel less than, doesn't it? This whole framework starts with the assumption that there's one right way for a brain to work, and yours missed the mark. It's like judging every animal by how well they climb trees - great for monkeys, not so much for dolphins.

This model does real damage. When everything about your neurotype gets framed as a problem to fix, you start believing you're fundamentally flawed. You spend all your energy trying to appear "normal" instead of developing your actual strengths. It's exhausting, and worse, it's completely backwards.

The traditional narrative goes something like this: You can't focus (except when you're hyperfocused to the point of forgetting to eat). You're too rigid (except when you're impulsively changing everything). You miss social cues (except when you're picking up on subtle patterns everyone else misses). See the problem? They're so busy looking at what you can't do, they miss the incredible things you can do.

Let's flip the script. **Your brain isn't failing at being neurotypical - it's succeeding at being neurodivergent.** That difficulty with task-switching? That's your brain's ability to achieve flow states most people only dream about. That tendency to see patterns everywhere? That's advanced pattern recognition that would make any data scientist jealous. That need for stimulation? That's your brain's hunger for novelty and innovation.

Marcus, an architect with AuDHD, spent years thinking he was terrible at his job because he couldn't do things the "normal" way. "I'd take three times longer than my colleagues to start a project because I needed to understand every single system involved. Then I'd hyperfocus and redesign everything seventeen times because my ADHD kept seeing new possibilities. My bosses thought I was inefficient." But when Marcus started his own firm and could work his own way, something amazing happened. His buildings won awards for innovative design that somehow felt perfectly integrated with their environments. His "inefficiency" was actually thoroughness combined with creative iteration.

The Synergy Effect: How Traits Amplify Rather Than Cancel Each Other

This is the part that really blows people's minds. Your autistic and ADHD traits don't cancel each other out. They amplify each other in ways that create entirely new capabilities. It's synergy in its purest form - the whole becomes greater than the sum of its parts.

Take hyperfocus. Neurotypicals think ADHD means you can't focus, and autism means you focus too much. But you? You've got both systems working together. Your ADHD interest-based nervous system latches onto something fascinating, and your autistic systematizing brain digs deep into every detail. The result? You can master complex subjects at speeds that seem impossible to others.

Or consider pattern recognition. Your autistic brain excels at spotting patterns and rules. Your ADHD brain makes lightning-fast connections between disparate concepts. Put them together, and you're seeing patterns across domains, making connections that revolutionize entire fields. You're not just following the breadcrumbs - you're seeing the entire forest from a perspective no one else has.

The social domain shows this synergy too. Yes, you might miss some neurotypical social cues. But you know what you don't miss? The patterns of behavior that reveal what people actually mean versus what they say. The inconsistencies in their stories. The subtle shifts in group dynamics. Your ADHD picks up on the energy changes, your autism catalogs the patterns, and suddenly you're understanding social situations at a deeper level than the people who "get" small talk.

Introducing the AuDHD Advantage Framework

So how do we harness all this potential? That's where the AuDHD Advantage Framework comes in. This isn't another coping strategy or masking technique. It's a complete reframe of how you understand and use your cognitive toolkit.

The framework has five core components:

1. The Interest Engine - Your combined ADHD dopamine-seeking and autistic special interest capacity creates an incredibly powerful learning system. When something captures both systems, you don't just learn about it - you absorb it at a molecular level.

2. The Pattern Matrix - Your ability to see patterns (autism) and make connections (ADHD) creates a unique form of intelligence. You're not just smart - you're smart in a way that sees through complexity to find elegant solutions.

4

3. The Innovation Loop - Your ADHD generates possibilities, your autism tests them against systematic understanding, creating a rapid prototyping system in your mind. You can iterate through solutions faster than most people can understand the problem.

4. The Truth Detector - Your autistic need for consistency combined with ADHD's alertness to novelty makes you incredibly good at spotting what's real versus what's performance. You see through the noise to find signal.

5. The Deep Dive Drive - When your ADHD interest and autistic systematizing align, you can go deeper into subjects than almost anyone else. You don't just become knowledgeable - you become an expert.

Self-Assessment: Mapping Your Unique Cognitive Profile

Now it's time to map your own unique cognitive profile. Every AuDHD brain is different, with its own specific blend of traits and capabilities. This isn't about scoring yourself against some arbitrary standard. It's about understanding your particular configuration.

Start by tracking your energy and attention patterns for a week. When do you hyperfocus? What triggers it? When does your brain feel like it's firing on all cylinders versus when it feels like you're pushing through mud? Don't judge these patterns - just observe them.

Notice your pattern recognition in action. What kinds of patterns jump out at you? Visual? Social? Systematic? Numerical? Narrative? Your brain has preferences, and knowing them helps you understand where your superpowers lie.

Pay attention to your innovation patterns too. How do ideas come to you? In torrents while you're doing something else? Through systematic analysis? In the intersection between two unrelated things? Your creative process is unique to you.

Track your special interests and hyperfocus topics. What subjects pull you in completely? What could you talk about for hours? What do you know at an almost encyclopedic level? These aren't just hobbies - they're windows into how your brain works best.

Finally, notice your truth detection in action. When do you spot inconsistencies? What kinds of lies or misrepresentations jump out at you immediately? This is your brain's quality control system at work.

Here's a practical exercise: Create a mind map of a recent hyperfocus session. Put the topic in the center. Branch out with all the connections you made, the patterns you spotted, the deep dives you took. Don't organize it - let it be as chaotic or systematic as it naturally wants to be. This map is a snapshot of your unique cognitive style in action.

Your Cognitive Toolkit in Action

Your AuDHD brain isn't a consolation prize. It's not a broken version of a "normal" brain. It's a finely-tuned system with capabilities that, once understood and properly utilized, can do things other brains simply can't. The question isn't how to fix your brain. The question is: Now that you understand what you're working with, what will you create?

Chapter 2: The Creative Engine

Where Deep Focus Meets Divergent Thinking

Your brain is doing something fascinating right now. While you're reading this, it's simultaneously tracking the main idea, making connections to your own experience, noticing patterns in how the information is presented, possibly getting distracted by a typo two paragraphs back, and generating three different project ideas based on something I haven't even said yet. This isn't chaos. This is your creative engine at work.

Most creativity researchers study either convergent thinking (finding the one right answer) or divergent thinking (generating multiple possibilities). But your AuDHD brain? It's running both programs simultaneously, creating a form of creativity that's almost impossible to replicate.

The Paradox of Simultaneous Depth and Breadth

Here's something that makes no sense to most people: You can be completely absorbed in intricate details while simultaneously seeing the big picture. You're examining individual trees with a magnifying glass while also mapping the entire forest from a satellite view. It sounds impossible, but you do it all the time.

This paradox happens because your autistic and ADHD traits aren't taking turns - they're working in parallel. Your autistic brain is diving deep, cataloging every detail, building comprehensive mental models. At the exact same time, your ADHD brain is scanning the horizon, making unexpected connections, jumping between levels of abstraction.

Emma, a software engineer, explains her experience: "When I'm debugging code, I'm simultaneously tracking the exact syntax error on line 247 and reconceptualizing the entire system architecture. My

7

brain is asking 'Why is this semicolon missing?' and 'What if we rebuilt this whole thing using a completely different paradigm?' at the same time. My neurotypical colleagues think I'm all over the place, but I'm actually holding both the microscopic and macroscopic view simultaneously."

This isn't multitasking in the traditional sense. You're not switching back and forth between depth and breadth. You're somehow doing both at once, creating a kind of dimensional thinking that lets you see problems from angles others can't even conceive of.

The practical result? You solve problems by going deeper than anyone else while also considering more alternatives than anyone else. You're not choosing between being a specialist or a generalist - you're both, simultaneously, in a way that creates entirely new possibilities.

Pattern Recognition Meets Rapid Association

Your pattern recognition abilities are off the charts, but not in the way most people think. It's not just that you see patterns - it's that you see patterns between patterns, meta-patterns, and patterns that haven't even emerged yet.

Your autistic brain excels at detecting rules, sequences, and systematic relationships. It's constantly running background processes, comparing everything against everything else you've ever noticed. Meanwhile, your ADHD brain is making associative leaps, connecting things that seem completely unrelated, finding similarities in the most unlikely places.

When these two systems work together, something magical happens. You're not just recognizing patterns - you're recognizing patterns across domains that most people keep completely separate. You see how the branching structure of rivers mirrors the branching in trees, blood vessels, and organizational hierarchies. You notice how the rhythm in a piece of music follows the same mathematical progression as population growth. You spot how social dynamics in your office mirror the territorial behaviors of the nature documentary you watched last night.

James, a data analyst with AuDHD, discovered a major fraud scheme that had gone undetected for years. "Everyone else was looking at the numbers in the spreadsheets. But I noticed that the timing of certain transactions matched the rhythm of someone's coffee breaks. Then I saw that the amounts followed a pattern similar to how my kid spreads peanut butter - starting thick and getting thinner. These weren't 'logical' connections, but my brain wouldn't let go of them. Turns out, the fraudster was literally entering fake transactions during their breaks, starting with bigger amounts when they were fresh and decreasing as they got tired."

This pattern-recognition-meets-association superpower means you're constantly generating insights that seem to come from nowhere. But they're not coming from nowhere - they're coming from your brain's unique ability to hold vast pattern libraries while simultaneously making wild associative leaps.

The "Productive Chaos" Model of Creativity

Let's talk about your creative process, because it probably drives you (and everyone around you) a little crazy. You've got seventeen browser tabs open, three different projects in various stages of completion, and you're simultaneously researching medieval blacksmithing techniques and modern quantum computing. This isn't disorganization - it's productive chaos.

The productive chaos model works like this: Your ADHD brain generates a massive variety of inputs, ideas, and connections. It's like someone turned on all the faucets at once. Meanwhile, your autistic brain is running quality control, pattern analysis, and systematic evaluation on everything that's flowing through. The chaos isn't random - it's carefully curated chaos.

Most creative processes are either generative (coming up with ideas) or evaluative (refining ideas). Yours is both, simultaneously, creating a kind of creative perpetual motion machine. You generate while you evaluate, evaluate while you generate, creating rapid iteration cycles that can produce innovations at stunning speed.

Here's what this looks like in practice. While working on one project, your ADHD brain notices something interesting in a completely unrelated domain. Instead of filing it away for later, your autistic brain immediately starts analyzing how it might apply to your current project. This triggers new associations in your ADHD brain, which your autistic brain then systematizes, which generates new possibilities, and round and round it goes.

Lisa, a graphic designer, describes her process: "I'll be designing a logo for a tech startup, and I'll have a cooking show on in the background. Suddenly I notice how the chef is plating the food in a spiral pattern, and my brain connects that to the golden ratio, which connects to the Fibonacci sequence in nature, which connects to shell structures, and boom - I've got a logo concept that represents growth, natural mathematics, and technological evolution. To everyone else, it looks like I'm not focusing. But that 'chaos' is actually my creative engine running at full capacity."

Case Studies: AuDHD Innovations That Changed Industries

The history of innovation is full of AuDHD minds that revolutionized entire fields by thinking differently. These aren't just success stories - they're blueprints for how your unique cognitive style can create breakthrough innovations.

Satoshi Tajiri, the creator of Pokémon, has been open about being on the autism spectrum and showing ADHD traits. As a child, he was obsessed with collecting insects (autistic special interest) but also constantly imagining new ways to categorize and battle them (ADHD creative generation). This combination led to a game concept that merged systematic collection with endless variety and exploration. Pokémon became the highest-grossing media franchise in history because it speaks to both the systematizing and novelty-seeking parts of the brain.

Temple Grandin revolutionized livestock handling by combining her autistic visual thinking and systematic analysis with creative problem-solving. She could simultaneously hold detailed mental models of how cattle move through spaces while also generating completely novel solutions. Her designs reduced stress in millions of animals because she could think like both an engineer and a cow.

Consider how **many unnamed innovators** in Silicon Valley show clear AuDHD traits. They create systems that are both elegantly systematic (appealing to the autistic brain) and endlessly variable (feeding the ADHD need for novelty). Think about how social media platforms combine rigid structure with infinite content variety, or how video games merge rule-based systems with creative exploration.

The pattern in all these innovations is clear: They succeed because they satisfy both the need for order and the need for novelty. They create systems that are simultaneously predictable and surprising, detailed and expansive, focused and flexible. Sound familiar? That's because they're products of minds like yours.

Exercise: Identifying Your Creative Sweet Spots

Time to map your own creative engine. This exercise will help you identify the conditions and contexts where your unique blend of deep focus and divergent thinking produces the best results.

Part 1: The Collision Journal For one week, keep track of your "collision moments" - times when two unrelated things suddenly connect in your mind. Write down:

- What you were supposedly focusing on

- What distracted you or caught your attention

- The unexpected connection you made

- Any insights or ideas that resulted

Don't judge these moments as "getting distracted." They're your creative engine at work.

Part 2: Environment Mapping Track your creative output in different environments:

- Silence versus background noise

- Organized space versus creative chaos

- Single-task versus multiple projects

- Morning versus evening

- Alone versus around others

You're looking for your optimal creative conditions. Maybe you need death metal playing while you do math. Maybe you need three projects running simultaneously to keep your brain engaged. There's no wrong answer - only your answer.

Part 3: The Interest Intersection Map List your top five special interests or hyperfocus areas. Now create a grid where each interest intersects with every other interest. In each intersection box, brainstorm what innovations might emerge from combining those two domains.

For example, if you're into both marine biology and music production, that intersection might generate ideas about using whale song patterns in electronic music, or creating underwater acoustics for aquariums that promote fish wellbeing, or developing synthesis techniques based on dolphin echolocation.

Part 4: Creative Flow Triggers Identify what triggers your best creative flow states:

- Specific types of challenges

- Certain times of day

- Particular kinds of deadlines (or lack thereof)

- Specific sensory inputs

- Social configurations

12

The goal isn't to force yourself into some "ideal" creative process. It's to understand your unique creative engine so you can work with it instead of against it.

Harnessing Your Creative Engine

Your creative engine doesn't run on the usual fuel. It needs complexity, multiplicity, depth, and breadth all at once. When you understand this and stop trying to force your brain into a neurotypical creative process, that's when the magic happens. Your simultaneous depth and breadth, your pattern-recognition-meets-association, your productive chaos - these aren't bugs in your system. They're features. Powerful ones.

Chapter 3: The Dual Processing Advantage

Something incredible happens in your brain when you look at any problem. Two processing systems fire up simultaneously, but they're not competing - they're collaborating in ways that create a unique form of intelligence. While everyone else is stuck choosing between forest or trees, you're seeing both, plus the ecosystem, the individual leaves, and probably three metaphorical connections to completely different domains.

This isn't a glitch. It's a gift. But like any powerful tool, you need to understand how it works to use it effectively. So let's dig into what's actually happening in that beautiful, complex brain of yours when both processing systems run at full capacity.

Bottom-up Detail Processing + Top-down Conceptual Thinking

Your brain processes information in two directions simultaneously, and this is where things get really interesting. Bottom-up processing starts with tiny details and builds toward understanding. Top-down processing starts with concepts and context, then fills in specifics. Most people rely heavily on one or the other. You? You're running both systems at full throttle.

Your autistic traits supercharge your bottom-up processing. You notice the individual pixels before seeing the picture. You hear each instrument in the orchestra separately. You spot the one misaligned icon in a sea of perfect uniformity. Your brain catalogs every detail, missing nothing, building comprehensive understanding from the ground up.

Meanwhile, your ADHD traits enhance your top-down processing. You grasp concepts instantly, see the big picture before anyone's even finished explaining, make intuitive leaps that turn out to be right. You understand the "why" before getting all the "whats." Your brain is constantly generating hypotheses, testing them against incoming information, adjusting on the fly.

When these systems work together? Magic. You're simultaneously building understanding from details up and from concepts down, meeting in the middle with insights nobody else could reach. It's like solving a puzzle from both edges and the middle at the same time.

Alex, a forensic accountant with AuDHD, explains: "When I look at financial records, I'm simultaneously tracking every single transaction (bottom-up) and sensing the overall pattern of fraud (top-down). I'll notice that three specific receipts have slightly different fonts - that's my detail processing. But I also immediately know something's wrong with the whole picture before I can explain why - that's my conceptual processing. When both systems agree something's off, I'm never wrong."

This dual processing means you catch things others miss at both levels. You spot the tiny inconsistencies that reveal big problems. You sense the conceptual issues that manifest in tiny details. You're running verification in both directions constantly.

Switching Between Microscope and Telescope Modes

Here's what nobody tells you about having both processing modes: You don't just have them, you can switch between them at will, or sometimes involuntarily, in ways that can be jarring to others but incredibly powerful when you harness them.

Microscope mode is when your autistic traits take the wheel. You zoom in so close you can see the atomic structure of the problem. Every detail becomes crystal clear. You notice things that are invisible to others because they're too zoomed out to see them. In this mode, you can spend hours perfecting a single paragraph, analyzing one data point, or understanding one mechanism.

Telescope mode is when your ADHD traits dominate. You zoom out so far you can see connections across galaxies of ideas. The details blur, but the patterns become obvious. You see trends, trajectories, possibilities. In this mode, you can redesign entire systems, revolutionize approaches, connect disparate fields.

But here's your superpower: You can switch between these modes rapidly, or even more remarkably, hold both simultaneously. It's like having a split screen in your brain - microscope on one side, telescope on the other.

The challenge? Sometimes the switching happens without your control. You're trying to finish a detailed task (microscope needed) but your brain keeps jumping to telescope mode, seeing all the ways the task connects to everything else. Or you're trying to brainstorm big picture strategy (telescope needed) but you get stuck on one tiny detail that's not quite right.

The "Zoom Lens" Technique for Problem-Solving

Since you have this incredible dual-processing capability, let's talk about how to use it intentionally. The zoom lens technique is a problem-solving approach that leverages your ability to shift between processing modes.

Start with telescope mode. Look at the problem from the highest level. What's the context? What are the ultimate goals? What patterns do you see? What does your intuition say? Don't worry about details yet - just get the lay of the land.

Now zoom in one level. What are the major components? How do they interact? What stands out as important? You're still in relatively telescope mode, but starting to see more structure.

Keep zooming in, level by level, until you hit microscope mode. Now you're looking at specific details, individual data points, particular mechanisms. What exactly is happening? What precisely is wrong? What specifically needs to change?

Here's the crucial part: Now zoom back out, but with all that detail loaded in your brain. As you zoom out, you'll see things you missed on the way in. The details inform the big picture, the big picture recontextualizes the details. Keep zooming in and out, and each pass reveals new insights.

Maria, a UX designer, uses this technique constantly: "When I'm designing an app interface, I start with the overall user journey (telescope), then zoom into specific screens, then into individual buttons and pixels, then back out to see how those pixels affect the journey. Each zoom level informs the others. I'll notice that a tiny animation delay (microscope) is ruining the entire flow (telescope), or that the overall concept (telescope) requires a specific detail (microscope) to work."

Managing the Toggle: When to Dive Deep vs. Scan Wide

The million-dollar question: How do you know when to use which mode? The answer isn't always obvious, and sometimes your brain decides for you. But with practice, you can get better at choosing the right mode for the right moment.

Signals you need microscope mode:

- Errors keep recurring despite big-picture solutions

- Something feels "off" but you can't articulate why

- You're in execution phase rather than planning phase

- Quality matters more than quantity

- You're learning something new that requires precision

Signals you need telescope mode:

- You're stuck on details that might not matter

- You need to prioritize or make strategic decisions

- You're in brainstorming or planning phase

- You need to communicate with big-picture thinkers

- You're feeling overwhelmed by complexity

The trick is recognizing when you're in the wrong mode for the task. If you're spending three hours choosing the perfect font for a presentation that's due in an hour, that's microscope mode when you need telescope. If you're making grand strategic plans without considering any practical details, that's telescope when you need microscope.

But here's a secret: Sometimes the "wrong" mode is exactly right. Your brain might force you into microscope mode on something seemingly trivial because it's detected something important. Or it might pull you into telescope mode during detail work because it's recognized a pattern that changes everything. Trust these instincts - they're usually onto something.

Practical Framework: The Focus-Flow Matrix

Let's make this practical with a framework you can actually use. The Focus-Flow Matrix helps you understand and optimize your dual processing based on two factors: task demands and your current brain state.

The Matrix:

High Focus Available + Detail Task Required = Pure Microscope Mode

- This is your sweet spot for detailed work

- Schedule critical detail work for these times

- Protect this time fiercely

High Focus Available + Big Picture Task Required = Controlled Zoom

- You can consciously switch between modes

- Perfect for strategic planning or system design

- Use the zoom lens technique here

Low Focus Available + Detail Task Required = Structured Microscoping

- Break details into tiny chunks

- Use external tools to track progress

- Accept that it'll take longer

Low Focus Available + Big Picture Task Required = Pure Telescope Mode

- Let your mind wander productively

- Great for brainstorming and connection-making

- Capture ideas without judging them

The key insight: **Stop fighting your current mode and start working with it.** If your brain wants telescope but the task needs microscope, either switch tasks or find a way to use telescope mode to inform the detailed work. If your brain's stuck in microscope but you need big picture, zoom in on a detail that represents the whole.

Rachel, a project manager with AuDHD, transformed her productivity with this framework: "I used to waste hours trying to force myself into the 'right' mode. Now I have a telescope task list and a microscope task list. When my brain wants to zoom out, I grab a telescope task. When it wants to dive deep, I grab a microscope task. My productivity tripled, and I stopped feeling like I was constantly fighting myself."

Your Dual Processing Superpower

Your ability to process information from both directions simultaneously isn't something to manage or cope with - it's something to celebrate and utilize. You have access to a form of intelligence that integrates detail and concept, trees and forest, microscope and telescope in ways that create genuinely new insights.

The world needs people who can see both the tiny cracks that could become major failures and the grand patterns that could become breakthrough innovations. That's you. Your dual processing advantage means you're equipped to solve problems that require both depth and breadth, detail and vision, precision and creativity.

So next time someone says you're too focused on details, or too scattered in your thinking, remember: You're not too anything. You're running sophisticated dual processing that they can't even imagine. And once you master the toggle, understand your patterns, and trust your instincts about when to zoom in or out? That's when you become unstoppable.

Chapter 4: Hyperfocus as a Superpower

Mastering Skills at Lightning Speed

You know that feeling when the entire world disappears? When time becomes meaningless, your body's needs fade away, and nothing exists except you and whatever has captured your complete attention? That state everyone else struggles to achieve through meditation apps and productivity hacks? You fall into it accidentally while researching vintage typewriter repair mechanisms at 2 AM.

This is hyperfocus - your brain's ability to achieve states of concentration so intense that neuroscientists are still trying to figure out how you do it. But here's what they miss: Your hyperfocus isn't just intense. It's qualitatively different. When your AuDHD brain locks onto something, it's running processes that other brains literally cannot access.

The Neuroscience of AuDHD Hyperfocus

Your hyperfocus is a neurological perfect storm, and understanding what's actually happening in your brain during these states is mind-blowing. It's not just "paying attention really hard." Your brain is doing something fundamentally different from neurotypical focus.

When neurotypical people focus, they're essentially turning up the volume on one channel while turning down others. It's like adjusting the balance on a stereo. But your AuDHD hyperfocus? It's more like your brain temporarily rewires itself to become a specialized processor for whatever you're focused on.

Your ADHD brain has an interest-based nervous system. Instead of being motivated by importance, rewards, or consequences like neurotypical brains, yours is motivated by interest, challenge, novelty,

21

and urgency. When something hits these triggers, your brain floods with dopamine and norepinephrine in patterns that are completely different from typical attention.

Meanwhile, your autistic brain brings its own superpowers to the party. The intense systematizing, the pattern recognition, the need to understand things completely - these traits create a depth of processing that goes beyond normal focus. Your brain doesn't just pay attention; it absorbs, categorizes, connects, and integrates information at a molecular level.

When these two systems combine in hyperfocus, something extraordinary happens. The ADHD brain provides the intense engagement and sustained attention (yes, ADHD brains can sustain attention when interested!). The autistic brain provides the systematic processing and deep understanding. Together, they create a learning state that's basically superhuman.

Research shows that during hyperfocus states, your brain shows unusual patterns of activation. The default mode network (usually associated with daydreaming) stays partially active while task-positive networks are fully engaged. You're simultaneously focused and making creative connections. Your brain is also showing increased connectivity between regions that don't usually talk to each other.

Dr. Rebecca Chen, a neuroscientist studying AuDHD cognition, puts it this way: "Most people's brains are like flashlights - they can direct a beam of attention. AuDHD brains in hyperfocus are like laser cutters - the intensity and precision are on a completely different scale."

Skill Acquisition on Steroids: The 100-Hour Mastery Principle

Here's something that'll blow your mind: While the famous "10,000-hour rule" suggests it takes that long to master a skill, many AuDHD individuals report reaching functional mastery in 100 hours or less when hyperfocusing. This isn't exaggeration - it's a different learning process entirely.

When you hyperfocus on learning something, you're not just practicing more. Your brain is encoding information differently. The combination of intense attention (ADHD) and systematic analysis (autism) creates accelerated learning curves that shouldn't be possible.

Take coding, for example. A neurotypical person might spend months learning a programming language, practicing an hour or two daily. You? You might disappear for a weekend, hyperfocus for 30 straight hours (with minimal breaks you won't remember taking), and emerge functional in that language. Not expert-level, but functional enough to build real things.

This happens because of how your brain processes during hyperfocus:

- **Compression learning**: You're taking in massive amounts of information and your pattern-recognition immediately starts finding connections and rules

- **Immediate application**: You don't learn theory then practice - you do both simultaneously

- **Deep encoding**: Information learned during hyperfocus gets encoded more deeply in memory

- **Systematic exploration**: You don't just learn the basics - you explore edge cases, exceptions, and variations

Marcus, a musician with AuDHD, learned to play piano to a performance level in three months: "I hyperfocused on piano for 8-10 hours a day. But it wasn't just practice. I was simultaneously learning music theory, analyzing the physics of sound, studying the biomechanics of hand movement, and recognizing patterns across different composers. My teacher said I learned differently than any student she'd had - like I was reverse-engineering the entire concept of piano from first principles while also training muscle memory."

The 100-hour principle works like this: When you hyperfocus on a skill for roughly 100 hours (this might be spread across a few weeks or compressed into days), you reach a tipping point. You've absorbed enough patterns, understood enough systems, and made enough connections that you can function independently in that domain. You're not a master yet, but you've compressed years of normal learning into weeks.

Creating Hyperfocus Triggers and Environments

Since hyperfocus is such a powerful tool, the obvious question is: Can you trigger it intentionally? The answer is yes, but not in the way productivity gurus would have you believe. You can't force hyperfocus, but you can create conditions where it's more likely to emerge.

Interest Inception: You can't fake interest, but you can find genuine interest triggers in almost anything. The key is finding the aspect that appeals to your specific brain. Hate accounting but need to learn it? Find the pattern-detection game within it. Bored by history? Focus on the systems and connections. Your brain needs a genuine hook, but that hook can be something others wouldn't even notice.

Environmental Architecture: Your sensory environment massively impacts your ability to enter hyperfocus. This is highly individual - some need absolute silence, others need death metal. Some need visual minimalism, others need controlled chaos. Track what environments have triggered hyperfocus before and recreate them.

The Pressure Sweet Spot: Too much pressure and your brain freezes. Too little and it won't engage. But there's a sweet spot where urgency meets interest that can trigger hyperfocus. This might be a deadline, a challenge from someone who doubts you, or a self-imposed constraint that makes things interesting.

Biological Priming: Your brain chemistry affects hyperfocus availability. Factors include:

- Sleep debt (some find mild sleep deprivation triggers hyperfocus, though this isn't sustainable)

- Caffeine (for some, it enhances hyperfocus; for others, it creates scattered attention)

- Exercise (many report that physical activity before mental work increases hyperfocus ability)

- Time of day (your brain has hyperfocus windows - usually late night or early morning)

The Rabbit Hole Method: Sometimes the best way to trigger hyperfocus is to give yourself permission to follow your curiosity without agenda. Start researching something mildly interesting and let yourself follow every tangent. Often, you'll hit something that triggers deep hyperfocus.

The Interest-Intensity Map: Predicting and Directing Your Focus

Not all interests are created equal when it comes to hyperfocus. Some topics trigger mild engagement, others activate your brain's nuclear reactor. Creating an Interest-Intensity Map helps you understand and predict your hyperfocus patterns.

Start by tracking your hyperfocus sessions for a month. Note:

- What triggered it (topic, challenge, question)

- Intensity level (1-10)

- Duration

- Productive output

- Recovery time needed

You'll start seeing patterns. Maybe certain types of problems (debugging code, solving mechanical puzzles, organizing systems) consistently trigger intense hyperfocus. Maybe certain domains (music theory, evolutionary biology, game mechanics) always capture you completely.

Plot these on a grid with Interest Type on one axis and Intensity on the other. You'll see clusters - your hyperfocus sweet spots. These are the areas where your brain naturally wants to go deep. This map becomes a powerful tool for directing your life and work toward domains where your hyperfocus gives you massive advantages.

Jennifer, a designer with AuDHD, discovered through mapping that her highest-intensity hyperfocus triggered on "systems with visual components" - information architecture, data visualization, user flow diagrams. She restructured her career toward these areas and became known as the person who could solve complex information design problems others couldn't even understand.

Warning Signs and Safety Valves: Healthy Hyperfocus Practices

Hyperfocus is powerful, but it's also dangerous if unmanaged. Your ability to ignore bodily needs, time, and the external world can lead to serious problems. You need safety valves - systems that protect you from the dark side of your superpower.

Physical Warning Signs:

- Dehydration headaches (you haven't drunk water in 8 hours)
- Bathroom urgency you've been ignoring
- Hunger that's turned into nausea
- Stiffness from not moving
- Eye strain from not blinking enough

Cognitive Warning Signs:

- Tunnel vision so narrow you're missing obvious solutions
- Repetitive actions that aren't producing progress
- Anger when interrupted (beyond normal frustration)
- Loss of temporal awareness (not knowing what day it is)

- Decision fatigue from too many micro-choices

Safety Valve Systems:

The External Circuit Breaker: Have someone you trust who can pull you out when needed. Give them permission to interrupt if you've been hyperfocusing beyond safe limits. This might be a partner, roommate, or even a timer-based check-in system.

The Biological Interrupt: Set up physical needs that force breaks. A small water bottle (requiring refills), a timer for stretches, a pet that demands attention. These create natural break points without completely breaking hyperfocus.

The Transition Protocol: Develop a routine for coming out of hyperfocus gently. Abrupt stops can be jarring and lead to hyperfocus hangovers. Try gradually widening attention - from the specific task to the project to the room to your body to the world.

The Recovery Ritual: After intense hyperfocus, your brain needs recovery. This might include: physical movement, social interaction, mindless activity, sensory regulation, or sleep. Treat this recovery as part of the hyperfocus cycle, not separate from it.

Using Hyperfocus Strategically

Your hyperfocus is like a superpower, but even superheroes need to use their powers wisely. You can't hyperfocus on everything, and you shouldn't try. Instead, deploy this ability strategically on things that matter, things that interest you, and things that benefit from the deep dive only you can achieve.

The world needs people who can disappear into problems and emerge with solutions. Who can learn entire domains in the time others learn basics. Who can see patterns and connections that become visible only through sustained, intense focus. That's you. Your hyperfocus isn't a symptom to manage - it's a gift to harness.

Chapter 5: The System Thinkers

Seeing Patterns Others Miss

There's something different about how you see the world. While others see individual events, isolated problems, and random occurrences, you see systems, patterns, and hidden connections. It's like everyone else is watching a movie while you're simultaneously seeing the script, the direction, the cinematography, and the underlying story structure.

This isn't just pattern recognition - it's system recognition. Your brain automatically maps relationships, spots inefficiencies, and detects inconsistencies in ways that feel like breathing to you but look like magic to others. And when this system-seeing ability combines with your justice sensitivity? You become someone who can't unsee the broken systems around you and feels compelled to fix them.

Justice Sensitivity Meets Systems Analysis

Your justice sensitivity isn't just about fairness - it's about systems that work correctly. When your autistic need for consistency meets your ADHD alertness to wrongness, you develop an almost allergic reaction to systems that don't function as they should.

This goes way beyond "that's not fair." You see the cascade effects of unfairness. You spot how one biased rule creates seventeen downstream problems. You notice when systems say they're doing one thing but are actually optimized for something completely different. It physically bothers you when systems are inefficient, inconsistent, or inequitable.

David, a policy analyst with AuDHD, describes it: "I can't just see that a law is unfair. I see the entire system that created it, the incentive structures that maintain it, and all the interconnected pieces that would need to change to fix it. It's like seeing a spider web where everyone else just sees a single thread."

Your justice sensitivity operates on multiple levels simultaneously:

- **Logical inconsistency**: Rules that contradict each other or their stated purpose

- **Systemic inefficiency**: Processes that waste resources or create unnecessary friction

- **Hidden inequity**: Systems that appear fair but create unequal outcomes

- **Structural violence**: How systems harm people through their normal operation

This multilevel analysis happens automatically. You don't choose to see these things - you can't NOT see them. It's like having X-ray vision for institutional bullshit.

The combination of justice sensitivity and systems analysis means you often understand problems better than the people in charge of solving them. You see not just what's broken, but why it's broken, what keeps it broken, and what would actually fix it (versus what would just look like fixing it).

The "Truth Detector": Spotting Inconsistencies and Inefficiencies

Your brain runs a constant background process that could be called "consistency checking." Every piece of information gets cross-referenced against everything else you know. When something doesn't match up, your brain throws an alert you can't ignore.

This truth detection operates through multiple mechanisms:

Pattern Violation Detection: Your autistic pattern recognition establishes baselines for how things typically work. When something violates these patterns, you notice immediately. This might be someone's behavior changing, data that doesn't fit the trend, or a story that doesn't follow logical sequence.

Multi-Point Verification: Your ADHD brain is simultaneously tracking multiple data streams. You're listening to what someone says while watching their body language while noting environmental context while remembering their past statements. When these don't align, you know something's off.

System Logic Analysis: You automatically map the logical structure of arguments, plans, and explanations. You see when conclusions don't follow from premises, when causes couldn't produce the claimed effects, when the pieces don't add up to the stated whole.

Sarah, a forensic accountant, explains her process: "I'll be reviewing financial documents and suddenly feel physically uncomfortable. Something's wrong, but I don't know what yet. So I start mapping the entire financial system - every transaction, every relationship, every pattern. Eventually, I find it: transactions that are technically legal but form a pattern that reveals fraud. My colleagues think I'm psychic. I'm not. I just can't ignore systemic inconsistencies."

This truth detection ability means you often know someone's lying before you know how you know. You sense inefficiencies before you can articulate them. You feel systemic problems in your bones before your conscious mind catches up.

From Pattern Recognition to Prediction

Here's where your system-thinking becomes almost prophetic: Once you understand a system's patterns, you can predict its future states with uncanny accuracy. Not because you're psychic, but because you see the underlying mechanisms others miss.

Your predictions work through several layers:

Trajectory Analysis: You see where systems are headed based on their current patterns. Like watching a ball arc through the air and knowing where it'll land, you see social, economic, and organizational trajectories others won't notice until impact.

Cascade Prediction: You understand how changes propagate through systems. When others see an isolated policy change, you see the domino effect it'll create across interconnected systems.

Pattern Completion: Your brain automatically completes partial patterns. You see where gaps will appear, where breaks will occur, where growth will happen, based on the system's inherent logic.

Cycle Recognition: You identify recurring patterns across different time scales. You notice that organizations, relationships, and even societies follow predictable cycles, and you can tell where in the cycle things currently are.

Tom, a business strategist with AuDHD, predicted his company's market crisis two years before it happened: "I saw the pattern in our customer data, the trajectory of our technology stack, and the cycle our industry was in. I wrote a detailed memo about what would happen and when. Leadership thought I was being dramatic. Two years later, everything I predicted came true, almost to the month. They called me a prophet. But I just saw where the system was naturally heading."

Turning System-Seeing into Career Advantages

Your ability to see and understand systems isn't just an interesting quirk - it's a massive career advantage when properly leveraged. The key is finding roles where system-thinking is valued and rewarded.

Natural Fit Careers:

- **Systems Architecture**: Designing complex technical or organizational systems

- **Strategic Analysis**: Predicting market trends, competitive dynamics, policy impacts

31

- **Process Optimization**: Finding inefficiencies and designing better workflows

- **Quality Assurance**: Spotting problems others miss before they become disasters

- **Research and Development**: Understanding complex problems and designing solutions

- **Forensic Analysis**: Detecting fraud, solving crimes, investigating failures

- **Urban Planning**: Understanding how city systems interact and impact each other

But here's the thing: You can apply system-thinking to any career. The trick is positioning yourself as the person who understands how things really work.

Marketing? You see customer behavior systems. Teaching? You understand learning systems. Art? You perceive aesthetic and cultural systems. Healthcare? You map treatment and outcome systems. There's no field where system-thinking isn't valuable.

The key is learning to translate your system insights into language others can understand and act on. You might see the whole system instantly, but others need it broken down into comprehensible pieces.

Tool: The Systems Mapping Technique

Let's make your system-seeing ability concrete with a technique you can use anywhere. The Systems Mapping Technique helps you visualize and communicate the patterns you naturally perceive.

Step 1: Identify System Components List every element in the system. Don't judge importance yet - just catalog everything you notice. People, processes, resources, rules, inputs, outputs, feedback loops.

Step 2: Map Relationships Draw connections between components. What influences what? What depends on what? What constrains what? Use different line types for different relationship types (causes, enables, prevents, requires).

Step 3: Identify Flows What moves through the system? Information? Money? Energy? Decisions? Track how these flows move and where they get stuck or accelerated.

Step 4: Find Feedback Loops Where does the system self-reinforce (positive feedback) or self-regulate (negative feedback)? These loops often drive system behavior more than individual components.

Step 5: Spot Leverage Points Where are the places where small changes could create big effects? These are usually found at loop intersections, flow bottlenecks, or rule-setting positions.

Step 6: Predict Patterns Based on the system's structure, what patterns would you expect? Where will problems emerge? Where will growth occur? What cycles will repeat?

Lisa used this technique to revolutionize her hospital's patient flow: "I mapped the entire emergency department system - not just the official workflow, but the actual system including unwritten rules, social dynamics, and resource constraints. I found seventeen feedback loops nobody knew existed. By changing just three small processes at key leverage points, we reduced wait times by 40% without adding any resources."

Your System-Seeing Superpower

Your ability to see systems isn't a burden, even though it can feel that way when you see broken systems everywhere. It's a rare gift that becomes more valuable as our world becomes more complex. While others are overwhelmed by complexity, you see through it to the underlying patterns.

Organizations need people who can see how things really work, not just how they're supposed to work. Who can predict problems before they manifest. Who can design solutions that actually solve problems rather than just appearing to. That's you.

Your justice sensitivity combined with systems analysis means you're not just seeing systems - you're seeing how they could be better. Your truth detection means you see through the stories organizations tell themselves to the reality of how they function. Your pattern recognition to prediction ability means you can guide organizations away from future problems and toward better futures.

Chapter 6: Rapid Prototyping Mind

Innovation Through Iteration

Your brain builds things differently than other brains. While everyone else is still planning, you've already built three versions in your head, tested them against reality, found the flaws, and started building version four. This isn't impulsiveness - it's rapid mental prototyping, and it's one of your greatest innovation advantages.

The combination of ADHD's "let's try it" impulse and autism's "let's perfect it" drive creates a unique innovation cycle. You don't just iterate quickly - you iterate with systematic purpose. Each version teaches you something essential, and your pattern recognition ensures you never make the same mistake twice.

The ADHD "Let's Try It" + Autistic "Let's Perfect It" Cycle

This cycle is the engine of your innovative capability, and understanding how it works changes everything about how you approach creative problems.

The ADHD side initiates. It sees a possibility and immediately wants to explore it. There's no lengthy deliberation, no paralysis by analysis. The idea appears, and your brain is already building. This isn't recklessness - it's rapid hypothesis generation. Your ADHD brain treats every idea as an experiment worth running.

Then the autistic side engages. It analyzes what you've built, spots every flaw, notices every inefficiency, sees every place where the system doesn't quite work. But instead of getting stuck in perfectionism, the ADHD side has already started building the next version, incorporating the autistic insights.

This creates a rapid cycling between generation and analysis, experimentation and systematization, creativity and criticism. Most people have to consciously switch between these modes. You're running both simultaneously.

Jake, a product designer with AuDHD, explains his process: "When I get a design brief, my brain immediately generates five different approaches. Not sequentially - simultaneously. Then my analytical side tears each one apart, finding the weak points. But while that's happening, I'm already generating versions 6 through 10, each incorporating the lessons from the analysis. By the time my neurotypical colleagues have finished their first sketch, I've mentally tested twenty variations."

The beauty of this cycle is that it's self-improving. Each iteration isn't just different - it's better, because your pattern recognition ensures you're learning from each version. You're not randomly trying things; you're systematically exploring the solution space.

Fail Fast, Analyze Deeply: The AuDHD Innovation Loop

"Fail fast" has become a Silicon Valley cliche, but your brain was doing it before it had a name. The difference is, you don't just fail fast - you fail smart. Every failure gets deeply analyzed, patterns extracted, lessons integrated.

Your innovation loop works in rapid spirals:

Generate: Your ADHD brain produces an idea or solution, often pulling from disparate domains.

Prototype: You build it mentally (or physically) just enough to test the core concept.

Test: You run it against your internal models of reality, checking for logical consistency, practical feasibility, system integration.

Analyze: Your autistic brain dissects what worked and what didn't, identifying specific failure points and success patterns.

Integrate: The lessons immediately feed into the next generation cycle.

Repeat: But now with all previous learnings integrated.

This loop can run incredibly fast - sometimes multiple complete cycles in minutes. You're not attached to any single solution because you know seventeen more are coming. This emotional detachment from individual ideas, combined with deep analytical learning from each one, creates innovation at machine-gun pace.

Amanda, a software architect, describes her innovation process: "When designing a new system, I'll 'build' and 'destroy' dozens of architectures in my mind before writing a single line of code. Each mental prototype teaches me something - this approach creates a bottleneck, that one has a security vulnerability, this other one doesn't scale. By the time I actually build something, I've learned from fifty failures nobody else even knows happened."

Building Minimum Viable Products in Your Head

You have an extraordinary ability: you can build and test products entirely in your mind. Not just imagine them - actually build them, complete with working parts, user interactions, failure modes, and edge cases.

This mental prototyping is possible because of how your brain processes information:

Systematic Modeling: Your autistic traits create detailed mental models of how things work. You don't just think about a product; you model its entire system.

Rapid Simulation: Your ADHD traits let you run quick simulations, playing out scenarios at high speed.

Pattern Library: Your vast library of observed patterns lets you predict how things will behave without physical testing.

Cross-Domain Integration: You pull solutions from completely unrelated fields, testing combinations others would never consider.

The result is that you can build, test, and refine products mentally at speeds that seem impossible. You're running a virtual R&D lab in your head 24/7.

Kevin, a game developer with AuDHD, created an award-winning game after mentally prototyping it for months: "I built the entire game in my head first. Every mechanic, every level, every player interaction. I could 'play' it mentally, finding where players would get stuck, where the difficulty ramped too fast, where the fun dropped off. When I finally built the actual game, it only took three weeks because I'd already solved all the problems in my head."

Case Studies: AuDHD Entrepreneurs and Their Iterations

Real AuDHD entrepreneurs show this rapid prototyping mind in action, creating innovations through relentless iteration rather than singular genius moments.

Case 1: The App Developer Rachel built a successful meditation app, but not in the way you'd expect. She started with 47 different concepts, built basic prototypes of each in a single weekend, tested them all on herself, identified the three with potential, combined their best features, and iterated through twelve more versions before launching. The final app looked nothing like any of the original 47, but contained DNA from all of them.

"People think I'm incredibly creative," Rachel says, "but I'm really just incredibly iterative. I don't have better ideas than anyone else - I just have more ideas, test them faster, and learn from them more systematically."

Case 2: The Restaurant Innovator Marcus revolutionized food delivery in his city, but through iteration, not inspiration. He started with a food truck, but used it as a testing laboratory. Every week, he'd try a different menu, different locations, different service models. His autistic pattern recognition tracked what worked; his ADHD drive kept generating new variations.

After 100 iterations, he'd discovered a unique model: ghost kitchens that could switch cuisines based on real-time demand data. "Everyone thought I was chaotic, constantly changing things. But I was systematically exploring the solution space. Each 'failure' taught me constraints and opportunities. The final business model was inevitable once I'd tested enough variations."

Case 3: The Educational Revolutionary Sam created an online learning platform that adapts to neurodivergent learning styles. The innovation came through relentless prototyping. She built seventeen different interface designs, twenty-three different curriculum structures, and forty-one different engagement mechanisms. Each version was tested, analyzed, and fed into the next iteration.

"My ADHD brain kept saying 'what if we tried this?' and my autistic brain kept saying 'here's why that didn't work,'" Sam explains. "Together, they created a learning platform that works for brains like mine because it was designed through the same iterative process our brains use naturally."

Framework: The Build-Test-Refine Protocol

Let's systematize your natural rapid prototyping ability into a framework you can consciously apply to any innovation challenge.

Phase 1: Divergent Building (ADHD leads)

- Generate multiple solutions without judgment

- Pull from different domains freely

- Build quick and dirty versions

- Focus on quantity over quality

- Time-box this phase to prevent endless generation

Phase 2: Systematic Testing (Autism leads)

- Test each prototype against specific criteria

- Document failure points precisely
- Identify patterns across failures
- Note unexpected successes
- Create a failure taxonomy

Phase 3: Integration Refinement (Both collaborate)

- Combine successful elements from multiple prototypes
- Apply failure lessons to new iterations
- Maintain what works while fixing what doesn't
- Test edge cases and extreme scenarios
- Build in redundancy for critical failure points

Phase 4: Pattern Recognition (Autism leads)

- Identify meta-patterns across all iterations
- Recognize solution families
- Spot convergent evolution (different approaches reaching similar solutions)
- Document design principles that emerge
- Create reusable solution templates

Phase 5: Creative Synthesis (ADHD leads)

- Combine patterns in novel ways
- Jump to non-obvious solutions based on learned principles
- Question assumptions revealed by testing
- Generate next-level iterations
- Push beyond local maxima

The key is not fighting your natural tendency to iterate rapidly. Instead, add just enough structure to capture learnings without slowing down the innovation cycle.

Practical Application Exercise: Choose a problem you're currently facing. Set a timer for 30 minutes. Generate and mentally test at least 10 different solutions. Don't develop any single solution for more than 3 minutes. Document only failure points and success patterns. After 30 minutes, synthesize learnings into version 11. This version will likely be better than anything you could have created through careful planning.

Your Rapid Prototyping Advantage

Your rapid prototyping mind is built for our current era. In a world that changes too fast for careful planning, your ability to iterate quickly while learning deeply is invaluable. While others are still perfecting their first attempt, you've learned from twenty failures and are building version twenty-one.

This isn't about being careless or unfocused. It's about recognizing that your brain is optimized for learning through doing rather than planning. Your innovations come not from singular moments of inspiration but from relentless iteration guided by systematic learning.

The future belongs to those who can adapt quickly while maintaining quality, who can experiment rapidly while learning deeply, who can fail fast while analyzing thoroughly. That's exactly what your brain is designed to do. Your rapid prototyping mind isn't just different - it's perfectly adapted for innovation in complex, fast-changing environments.

Chapter 7: Profiles in AuDHD

Learning from the Innovators

Success leaves clues. And when you look at the patterns of successful AuDHD individuals across different fields, those clues become a roadmap. These aren't just inspiring stories (though they are that too). They're blueprints for how to leverage your unique cognitive wiring to create breakthroughs in any field.

What you'll notice in these profiles isn't perfection. None of these people "overcame" their AuDHD traits. Instead, they built their success around them, through them, because of them. They found ways to make their restlessness productive, their obsessions profitable, their system-seeing revolutionary.

The Scientist Who Couldn't Sit Still: Research Breakthroughs Through Restlessness

Dr. Maya Chen's lab doesn't look like other neuroscience labs. There's a treadmill desk, three different workstations, and what she calls her "thinking hammock." Her research assistants know that meetings might happen while she's walking circles around the building. They also know that this apparent chaos has produced three major breakthroughs in understanding neural plasticity.

"Everyone told me I'd never make it in science because I couldn't sit still through lectures," Maya explains. "They were right about the sitting still part. Wrong about everything else."

Maya's ADHD means she needs movement to think. But instead of fighting this, she built her entire research methodology around it. She designs experiments while walking, analyzes data while bouncing on an exercise ball, and has her best insights during what she calls "productive pacing."

Her autistic traits bring the systematic rigor. She's developed intricate organizational systems that let her track hundreds of variables across multiple experiments. Her pattern recognition is so acute that she spotted connections between seemingly unrelated neural pathways that had been missed for decades.

The breakthrough that made her famous came from this combination. While pacing during data analysis (ADHD in action), she noticed a pattern in neural firing sequences (autism's pattern recognition) that reminded her of ant colony behavior she'd observed during a hyperfocus rabbit hole about social insects (AuDHD's unexpected connections).

This led to her revolutionary discovery: neurons organize themselves using similar algorithms to social insects. This insight has transformed how we understand brain injury recovery and opened entirely new treatment pathways.

"My restlessness isn't a distraction from my work," Maya says. "It's an essential part of my thinking process. Movement generates connections. The key was designing a research environment that works with my brain, not against it."

Her advice for other restless scientists: "Your body knows what your brain needs. If you need to move to think, then movement is part of your scientific method. The biggest breakthroughs come from brains that work differently. Science needs your different."

The Artist Who Sees in Systems: Creating Worlds Through Pattern and Chaos

Jordan Blake's art doesn't fit in any traditional category. It's part installation, part algorithm, part living system. Gallery owners initially didn't know what to do with pieces that changed based on viewer interaction, weather patterns, and stock market data. Now they're in museums worldwide.

"I see systems everywhere," Jordan explains. "Social systems, natural systems, mathematical systems. My art makes these invisible systems visible."

Jordan's autistic pattern recognition means they see structures others miss. The way crowds move through spaces follows predictable patterns. Color relationships follow mathematical rules. Even chaos has its own systematic beauty. Their ADHD adds the creative chaos - the willingness to combine systems that shouldn't go together, to break patterns just to see what happens.

Their most famous piece, "Emergence," started as a hyperfocus on murmuration patterns in starlings. Jordan spent three months studying, filming, and analyzing bird flocks. But the ADHD brain made connections: these patterns appeared in stock trading algorithms, in social media information spread, in protest movements.

The final piece is an interactive installation where viewers' movements generate visual patterns based on flocking algorithms, but modified by real-time data from financial markets and social media. The result is beautiful, unsettling, and reveals hidden connections between natural and human systems.

"My autistic brain sees the rules," Jordan says. "My ADHD brain breaks them. Together, they create art that's both systematic and chaotic, predictable and surprising."

Jordan's studio practice embraces both sides. Intense hyperfocus sessions where they might work for 20 hours straight, followed by periods of apparent chaos where they're working on twelve pieces simultaneously. They've learned not to fight either mode but to prepare for both.

The Entrepreneur Who Debugs Reality: Building Businesses from Special Interests

Alex Rodriguez built a billion-dollar company from a childhood obsession with organizational systems. Not despite being AuDHD, but because of it.

"I was that kid who reorganized my Halloween candy seventeen different ways," Alex laughs. "Turns out, that's a marketable skill."

Alex's company creates organizational software, but not the boring kind. It's software that thinks like an AuDHD brain - allowing for multiple organizational systems simultaneously, adapting to changing priorities, making patterns visible. It's organization for people whose brains don't fit into traditional systems.

The journey wasn't smooth. Alex started and abandoned six different businesses before finding the right fit. But each "failure" taught crucial lessons. The ADHD impulsivity meant starting quickly, the autistic analysis meant understanding exactly why each attempt failed.

"My special interest is systems optimization," Alex explains. "But my ADHD means I see opportunities everywhere. The combination is powerful - I can spot inefficiencies instantly and imagine seventeen ways to fix them."

The breakthrough came when Alex realized they weren't the only one struggling with traditional organizational tools. Neurotypical productivity systems assume brains that work in ways AuDHD brains don't. So Alex built tools for brains like theirs - tools that embrace multiple parallel projects, that allow for hyperfocus and scattered attention, that make patterns visible while allowing for creative chaos.

The company culture reflects Alex's neurotype. Employees can work whenever they're most productive. Meetings are walking meetings or stand-up meetings. The office has quiet zones and chaos zones. It's designed for neurodivergent productivity.

"I'm not debugging software," Alex says. "I'm debugging reality - finding where the world's systems don't work for brains like ours and building better ones."

The Activist Who Won't Compromise: Changing Systems Through Persistent Vision

Sam Washington has been called stubborn, inflexible, and impossible to work with. They've also successfully changed three major policies in their city and influenced national legislation. Their secret? AuDHD traits that make them incapable of accepting unjust systems.

"I literally cannot let go of injustice," Sam explains. "My brain won't stop processing it until it's fixed."

Sam's autism means they see systems with brutal clarity - every inefficiency, every inequity, every place where stated values don't match actual outcomes. Their ADHD provides the energy and urgency to act on what they see. Together, these traits create an activism style that's relentless, systematic, and surprisingly effective.

Their first major victory came from hyperfocusing on their city's housing policy. Sam spent six months analyzing every aspect of the system, creating detailed maps of how policies created homelessness, building models that showed exactly how different changes would play out.

"Everyone else was having philosophical debates about housing," Sam says. "I was doing math. I showed them exactly how their current system was designed to fail and exactly what would fix it."

Sam's advocacy style is unique. They info-dump data at city council meetings. They create visualization systems that make complex injustices impossible to ignore. They can't do small talk at political events, but they can explain systemic problems with such clarity that even opponents have to listen.

The autism means they won't compromise on core principles, which others see as inflexibility but is actually moral clarity. The ADHD means they're always finding new angles of attack, new ways to present information, new coalitions to build.

"My brain is wired for justice," Sam says. "I see systems that hurt people, and I can't not try to fix them. It's not a choice - it's how my brain works."

Common Threads: Extracting Success Principles

Looking across these profiles, clear patterns emerge. These aren't rules to follow but principles to adapt to your own unique configuration of traits.

Principle 1: Build Around Your Traits, Not Despite Them Every successful AuDHD person structured their life to work with their neurotype. Maya built a lab that accommodates movement. Jordan created an art practice that embraces both hyperfocus and chaos. Alex designed a company culture around neurodivergent productivity. Sam turned their inability to accept injustice into a superpower.

Principle 2: Special Interests Are Professional Advantages What seems like obsession to others is actually deep expertise. Maya's random hyperfocus on ants led to breakthrough neuroscience. Jordan's system-seeing became their artistic signature. Alex's organization obsession became a billion-dollar business. Sam's fixation on justice made them an unstoppable advocate.

Principle 3: Synthesis Is the Superpower The magic happens when ADHD and autistic traits work together. ADHD provides energy and connections; autism provides depth and system-understanding. Success comes from letting both operate fully rather than suppressing either.

Principle 4: Iteration Beats Perfection Every profile includes multiple "failures" that were actually iterations. The ADHD drives trying new things; the autism analyzes what worked and what didn't. Success comes from rapid iteration with systematic learning.

Principle 5: Different Is the Advantage None of these people succeeded by being better at neurotypical approaches. They succeeded by doing things in ways that only AuDHD brains can do. The difference isn't a barrier to overcome - it's the competitive advantage.

Your Innovation Blueprint

These aren't just success stories. They're proof that your brain's unique wiring is designed for innovation. Your restlessness can drive research breakthroughs. Your system-seeing can create revolutionary art. Your special interests can build businesses. Your inability to accept broken systems can change the world.

The key isn't to follow someone else's path but to understand the principles and apply them to your own unique interests, talents, and traits. Your success won't look like anyone else's because your brain doesn't work like anyone else's. And that's exactly the point.

Chapter 8: The Interest Ecosystem

Building a Life Around Your Passions

Your interests aren't hobbies. They're not distractions. They're not "obsessions" that need to be managed. They're the architecture of your cognitive operating system, and when you build your life around them instead of fighting them, everything changes.

Most people have interests. You have special interests - intense, consuming, systematic explorations that rewire your brain and reshape your reality. The neurotypical world tells you to "balance" these interests, to "not get too focused on one thing." But what if the opposite is true? What if your special interests are supposed to be the center of your life, not the periphery?

Special Interests as Career Foundations

Here's a radical truth: Your special interests aren't separate from your career potential - they ARE your career potential. Every random hyperfocus, every "weird" obsession, every deep dive that seems completely impractical? They're building blocks for professional success that only you can achieve.

Special interests work differently in AuDHD brains. Your autism drives you to understand things completely, systematically, from every angle. Your ADHD connects these interests to unexpected domains, finds novel applications, sees possibilities others miss. Together, they create expertise that goes beyond normal specialization.

Consider Marcus, who spent his teenage years obsessed with speedrunning video games - playing games as fast as possible by finding exploits and optimizing every movement. His parents worried he was wasting his life. Today, he's a highly paid process optimization consultant. Those years of speedrunning trained his brain to see inefficiencies, find shortcuts, and optimize systems. The "useless" hobby was actually intensive training in a highly marketable skill.

Or Emma, whose special interest in Victorian death customs seemed morbid and impractical. She now runs a successful business helping families create meaningful, personalized memorial services. Her deep understanding of how different cultures approach death, combined with her systematic knowledge of ritual and meaning-making, created a unique professional niche.

Your special interests build several types of career capital:

Deep Expertise: You don't just learn about your interests - you absorb them at a molecular level. This creates expertise that can't be faked or fast-tracked.

Cross-Domain Connections: Your ADHD brain connects your special interests to everything else, creating unique interdisciplinary insights.

Problem-Solving Frameworks: Each special interest teaches you different ways of thinking that you can apply to other challenges.

Authentic Passion: You can't fake the energy that comes from working in your special interest area, and that authentic enthusiasm is magnetic.

The Passion-Profession Pipeline

Building a career from special interests isn't always straightforward, but there's a pipeline - a process for transforming passion into profession. It doesn't happen overnight, but it does happen.

Stage 1: Pure Exploration This is where you're just following your interest without any professional intention. You're learning for the joy of learning, exploring because you can't help yourself. Don't rush this stage. The depth you develop here becomes your professional foundation.

Stage 2: Skill Recognition Start identifying the meta-skills you're developing. If your special interest is medieval architecture, you're not just learning about buildings. You're developing skills in structural analysis, historical research, 3D visualization, and systems thinking.

Stage 3: Connection Making Your ADHD brain naturally does this - finding connections between your special interest and real-world problems. Medieval castle defense strategies apply to cybersecurity. Pokemon breeding mechanics relate to genetic algorithms. Train scheduling systems inform supply chain management.

Stage 4: Value Translation Figure out how your special interest knowledge solves problems people will pay to have solved. This isn't about abandoning your interest - it's about finding where your deep knowledge meets market needs.

Stage 5: Niche Creation Often, the perfect job for your special interest combination doesn't exist yet. So you create it. You become the medieval architecture consultant for video game companies, the Pokemon-genetics educator, the train-enthusiast supply chain optimizer.

Lisa's journey through this pipeline is instructive. Her special interest in fonts seemed completely unemployable. But through the pipeline, she recognized she'd developed skills in visual pattern recognition, historical research, and cultural analysis. She connected typography to brand identity and user experience. She translated this into value by showing companies how font choices影响 customer behavior. Now she's a typography consultant earning six figures helping brands choose fonts that align with their values and connect with their audiences.

Creating Sustainable Interest Cycles

One challenge with special interests is sustainability. The intensity that makes them powerful can also lead to burnout. The key is creating cycles that allow for both intense engagement and recovery.

The Seasonal Model: Some people with AuDHD find their interests naturally cycle with seasons. Summer might be your building season, winter your research season. Instead of fighting these cycles, structure your year around them.

The Spiral Model: Instead of moving linearly through interests, you spiral back to previous ones with new perspective. Each return adds depth. Your childhood interest in dinosaurs becomes paleontology becomes evolutionary biology becomes systems theory, each loop adding layers.

The Web Model: Multiple interests interconnect, creating a web where engaging with one strengthens others. Your interests in cooking, chemistry, and teaching combine into food science education. No interest exists in isolation.

The Phoenix Model: Some interests need to completely burn out before they can regenerate. This isn't failure - it's a natural cycle. The interest will return transformed, often when you least expect it.

Kevin uses the Web Model with five interconnected interests: music production, mathematics, teaching, coding, and philosophy. "They feed each other," he explains. "Math informs my music. Music teaches me about patterns I apply to coding. Coding gives me tools for teaching. Teaching makes me think philosophically. Philosophy brings me back to math. I'm never bored because I can switch interests while staying in the same conceptual space."

Monetizing Your Obsessions Ethically

There's a fear that monetizing special interests will ruin them. And done wrong, it can. But done right, it creates sustainable ways to spend more time with what you love.

Keep Sacred Spaces: Not every aspect of your special interest needs to be monetized. Keep some parts just for joy. If you love trains, maybe you monetize your knowledge of train systems but keep your model train collection as pure hobby.

Value-Aligned Monetization: Only monetize in ways that align with why you love the interest. If you love teaching others about your interest, monetization through education feels natural. If you love the solitary exploration, forcing yourself to teach might kill the joy.

Multiple Revenue Streams: Don't put all pressure on one aspect. Maybe you write about your interest, consult on it, create products related to it, and teach it. Diversification protects both income and joy.

The 80/20 Rule: Aim to monetize 20% of your special interest time, keeping 80% for pure exploration. This maintains the joy while creating sustainability.

Rachel found the balance with her special interest in coral reefs. "I monetize through scientific illustration and educational content, which feels aligned with my values of conservation. But my actual reef diving and research stays non-commercial. That separation keeps both sides healthy."

Worksheet: Mapping Your Interest Ecosystem

Time to map your own interest ecosystem. This isn't about choosing one interest to focus on - it's about understanding how all your interests interconnect and support each other.

Part 1: Interest Inventory List every significant interest you've had, past and present. Include:

- Childhood obsessions
- Academic fascinations
- "Failed" career attempts
- Current hyperfocuses
- Dormant interests that might reactivate

Part 2: Skill Mining For each interest, identify:

- Technical skills developed

- Thinking patterns learned

- Problem-solving approaches gained

- Knowledge domains mastered

- Connections to other fields noticed

Part 3: Connection Mapping Draw lines between interests that connect. How does your interest in architecture relate to your love of strategy games? How does your fascination with weather patterns connect to your interest in emotional regulation? You'll be surprised how interconnected everything is.

Part 4: Value Identification For each interest or interest cluster, identify:

- Problems it could solve

- People it could help

- Knowledge gaps it could fill

- Innovations it could inspire

- Systems it could improve

Part 5: Sustainability Planning For each interest, determine:

- What parts stay sacred (non-monetized)

- What parts could create value for others

- What cycle pattern it follows (seasonal, spiral, web, phoenix)

- What recovery/restoration it needs

- How it feeds other interests

Part 6: Next Steps Choose one interest intersection to explore professionally. Not abandoning others - just starting somewhere. What's the smallest step toward value creation you could take this week?

Your Interest-Powered Future

Your special interests aren't distractions from your "real" life - they're the blueprint for it. They're not obsessions to be managed but powers to be harnessed. When you stop fighting them and start building around them, you create a life that doesn't just accommodate your neurodiversity but is powered by it.

The world needs specialists who go deeper than anyone else thought possible. It needs connectors who see relationships others miss. It needs people whose authentic passion for seemingly obscure topics reveals universal truths. That's you. Your interests aren't too narrow, too weird, or too intense. They're exactly right for the unique contribution only you can make.

Chapter 9: Communication Superpowers

Direct, Authentic, and Revolutionary

You've been told your whole life that you communicate wrong. Too direct. Too much information. Too intense. Missing the point. Not getting the hint. But what if your communication style isn't wrong - it's revolutionary? What if the world desperately needs people who say what they mean, share information generously, and cut through the layers of social performance to reach actual truth?

Your AuDHD communication style might not fit neurotypical norms, but it has powers that most people can't access. When you learn to harness these powers instead of hiding them, you become a communication force that can transform every interaction, relationship, and system you touch.

The Gift of Directness in a World of Subtext

Neurotypical communication is exhausting. It's layers upon layers of subtext, hidden meanings, political correctness, and unspoken rules. People say one thing while meaning another, agree when they disagree, smile when they're angry. It's a constant performance that prioritizes social harmony over truth.

You can't do this. Not won't - can't. Your autistic brain needs clarity and consistency. Your ADHD brain doesn't have the patience for social theater. Together, they create a communication style that's direct, clear, and refreshingly honest.

"I spent years thinking I was bad at communication," shares David, a project manager with AuDHD. "Then I realized - I'm excellent at communication. I'm just bad at the neurotypical performance of pretending to communicate while actually obscuring information."

Your directness has several superpowers:

Clarity Creation: In a world drowning in corporate speak and political correctness, your ability to say exactly what you mean is revolutionary. You cut through confusion and get to the point.

Trust Building: While directness can initially shock people, those who stick around learn they can trust you completely. You say what you mean. No games, no hidden agendas.

Problem Identification: You name problems others are too polite to mention. That elephant in the room everyone's ignoring? You point right at it and say, "Hey, there's an elephant here."

Efficiency Maximization: Your direct communication saves enormous time and energy. While others spend hours dancing around issues, you've already identified the problem and proposed three solutions.

But directness needs framing to be effective. It's not about being harsh - it's about being clear. Here's how to harness your directness as a superpower:

Lead with Intent: "I'm going to be direct because I respect you too much to waste your time..."

Acknowledge the Style: "I tend to communicate very directly. Please know it comes from a place of wanting clarity and efficiency..."

Invite Reciprocity: "I appreciate direct communication. Please don't feel you need to soften things for me..."

Provide Context: "The neurotypical approach would be to hint at this for three meetings. I'm just going to say it..."

Info-Dumping as Teaching Superpower

Info-dumping - that thing where you share everything you know about a topic in an enthusiastic flood of information - is supposedly a social sin. But reframed, it's actually a teaching superpower.

When you info-dump, you're not just sharing facts. You're:

- Modeling passionate learning
- Providing comprehensive context
- Making connections visible
- Sharing your cognitive process
- Inviting others into your world of intense interest

The problem isn't info-dumping itself - it's the mismatch between your comprehensive sharing style and neurotypical attention patterns. The solution isn't to stop info-dumping but to channel it effectively.

The Teaching Transform: Position yourself in roles where info-dumping is valued. Teaching, training, consulting, writing, creating content - these are spaces where your comprehensive knowledge sharing is exactly what's needed.

Sarah, a cybersecurity consultant, turned her info-dumping into a career advantage: "Clients hire me because I'll tell them everything about their security vulnerabilities. Every detail, every connection, every possible scenario. What others call 'too much information,' my clients call 'thorough analysis.'"

The Enthusiasm Amplifier: Your authentic excitement when info-dumping is contagious. People might not remember all the facts, but they remember your passion. This makes you memorable and inspiring.

The Context Creator: Your comprehensive sharing provides context others miss. While neurotypical communication often lacks sufficient background, you provide the full picture, helping people understand not just what but why.

To make info-dumping more accessible:

Check In Periodically: "I'm about to go deep on this - are you ready for the full download?"

Offer Levels: "I can give you the headline, the summary, or the full deep dive - what would be helpful?"

Create Structure: "Let me share three key things about this, and each has several fascinating aspects..."

Invite Interaction: "Stop me if you want me to go deeper on any part..."

Building Bridges Between Neurotypes

Your communication style can actually bridge the gap between neurotypes. Because you process information differently, you can translate between different cognitive styles in ways others can't.

Your autistic pattern recognition helps you decode neurotypical subtext patterns. Your ADHD connectivity helps you find analogies that make complex ideas accessible. Together, they make you a natural translator between different ways of thinking.

The Pattern Decoder: You can learn neurotypical communication patterns the same way you learn any system. Once you see the patterns, you can translate between direct and indirect communication.

The Explicit Educator: You naturally make implicit things explicit, which helps everyone communicate better. You name unspoken rules, identify hidden assumptions, question unclear norms.

The Alternative Provider: You offer different ways of understanding things. Your unique perspective helps others see solutions they couldn't imagine.

Michael, a team facilitator with AuDHD, describes his bridge-building: "I'm like a communication interpreter. When the neurotypical folks are being too indirect, I translate for the neurodivergent team members. When the neurodivergent folks are being too direct, I help frame it for the neurotypicals. I can see both systems, so I can help them talk to each other."

Creating Your Communication Style Guide

Instead of masking your communication style, create a guide that helps others understand and work with it. This isn't about changing who you are - it's about creating an interface between your style and the world.

Your Communication Operating Manual:

How I Process Information:

- I need specific, concrete information rather than vague suggestions
- I take things literally, so please say what you mean
- I process better with written communication I can review
- I might need time to process before responding

How I Share Information:

- I tend to be comprehensive and detailed
- I share context and connections others might not mention
- I communicate directly without hidden meanings
- My enthusiasm might seem intense but it's genuine

What Works Best:

- Clear, explicit communication
- Permission to ask clarifying questions
- Patience with processing time
- Appreciation for thoroughness

What Doesn't Work:

- Hints, subtle cues, or indirect suggestions
- Assumed context or unspoken rules

- Pressure for immediate responses

- Criticism of communication style rather than content

Scripts and Frameworks for Common Scenarios

Having scripts and frameworks ready makes communication easier and less exhausting. These aren't masks - they're tools that help you communicate authentically while meeting social needs.

The Meeting Contribution Framework: "I have a comprehensive thought on this. Would it be helpful if I shared the full analysis, or should I start with the summary?"

The Social Event Survival Script: "I'm genuinely interested in what you're sharing, but I process better with specific topics. Could you tell me more about [specific aspect]?"

The Conflict Resolution Format: "I want to address this directly because I value our relationship. Here's what I observed... Here's how it affected me... Here's what would work better for me... What would work for you?"

The Boundary Setting Statement: "I communicate most effectively when I can be direct and thorough. If that style doesn't work for you, let's find a different way to exchange information that works for both of us."

The Info-Dump Introduction: "I'm really passionate about this topic and have lots to share. Would you like the highlights, or are you up for the deep dive?"

The Processing Time Request: "That's an important question and I want to give you a thoughtful answer. Can I take some time to process and get back to you?"

The Clarification Seeking Script: "I want to make sure I understand correctly because I sometimes miss subtext. Are you saying [explicit interpretation]?"

Your Revolutionary Communication

Your communication style isn't a deficit to be corrected. It's a revolutionary force in a world drowning in indirect, unclear, inauthentic communication. Your directness cuts through confusion. Your info-dumping shares knowledge generously. Your authenticity builds real trust.

The world needs people who say what they mean. Who share information enthusiastically. Who ask the questions everyone's thinking but not saying. Who make the implicit explicit. That's you. Your communication style might not fit the neurotypical norm, but that's exactly why it's so valuable.

When you stop apologizing for how you communicate and start leveraging it as the superpower it is, you become a force for clarity, authenticity, and truth in every space you enter. You're not bad at communication - you're revolutionary at it.

Chapter 10: Environmental Architecture

Designing Your Success Space

Your environment isn't just where you exist - it's part of your cognitive system. For AuDHD brains, the difference between a supportive environment and a hostile one can be the difference between thriving and barely surviving. But here's what most people don't understand: the "perfect" environment for you might look completely wrong to everyone else.

You're not being difficult when fluorescent lights make you want to crawl out of your skin. You're not being dramatic when the wrong texture sends your whole system into revolt. You're not being antisocial when you need to control your sensory input. Your brain processes environmental information differently, more intensely, and that's not a weakness - it's just a different operating system that needs different settings.

Sensory Optimization for Peak Performance

Your sensory system is like a mixing board with all the knobs turned to extreme settings. Some inputs are cranked to eleven, others are barely registering. Understanding your unique sensory profile is the first step to creating environments where you can actually function, let alone excel.

Visual Environment: Your visual processing might be hypersensitive to certain wavelengths, patterns, or movements. Fluorescent lights might feel like strobe lights to your brain. Cluttered spaces might overwhelm your processing capacity. Or conversely, you might need visual stimulation - blank walls might feel like sensory deprivation.

James, a software developer with AuDHD, discovered his productivity tripled when he replaced overhead lighting with multiple adjustable lamps using warm LED bulbs. "It wasn't just comfort," he explains. "My brain was using so much processing power to deal with the fluorescent flicker that I had nothing left for coding. Change the lights, free up the processing power."

Auditory Landscape: You might hear the electricity humming in the walls, the conversation three offices over, the HVAC system cycling. Or you might need sound to focus - silence might be deafening. The key is understanding what your brain does with auditory information.

Some AuDHD people need brown noise to mask distracting sounds. Others need specific music - not for enjoyment, but as cognitive scaffolding. Sarah works with death metal playing because "the complexity occupies the part of my brain that would otherwise be creating distractions."

Tactile Territory: Texture matters more than neurotypicals can imagine. The wrong fabric might make concentration impossible. The right fidget tool might make focus possible. Your skin is part of your thinking apparatus.

Olfactory Optimization: Smells can either ground you or completely derail you. Some AuDHD people find certain scents help with transitions or focus. Others need completely neutral environments. That "nice" air freshener in the office might be cognitive kryptonite for you.

Proprioceptive Needs: Your body's sense of itself in space affects everything. You might need weight (weighted blankets, compression clothing), movement (standing desk, balance ball), or specific positions to think clearly.

The Goldilocks Zone: Finding Your Just-Right Stimulation Level

Here's the paradox: You need more stimulation than neurotypicals to stay engaged, but you also get overwhelmed more easily. It's not contradiction - it's complexity. You need the *right* stimulation at the *right* level at the *right* time.

Your Goldilocks Zone shifts based on:

- Time of day

- Current stress levels

- Recent sensory exposure

- Task demands

- Social battery level

- Special interest activation

The zone for deep focus work might be completely different from the zone for creative brainstorming or social interaction. This isn't inconsistency - it's sophisticated environmental matching.

Maria maps her zones: "Morning focus needs silence, afternoon creativity needs coffee shop noise, evening planning needs nature sounds. It took me years to stop forcing myself into the wrong zones at the wrong times."

Creating adjustable environments is key. Instead of one fixed setup, you need options:

- Lighting that dims and changes color temperature

- Sound options from silence to brown noise to metal music

- Seating options from desk to floor to walking

- Temperature control (even if it's just a fan and a heating pad)

- Visual options from minimalist to stimulating

Digital Environments and Tool Stacks for AuDHD Minds

Your digital environment is as important as your physical one. The wrong interface can make tasks impossible; the right one can make you superhuman.

Visual Interface Optimization:

- Dark modes aren't just preference - they might be necessity

- Font choices affect processing speed

- Color coding can offload cognitive work

- Multiple monitors allow for peripheral information without task-switching

Notification Management: Your ADHD wants all the notifications (novelty! dopamine!). Your autism wants predictability and control. The solution isn't all or nothing - it's intelligent filtering.

Kevin uses a three-tier system: "Emergency notifications get through always. Work notifications only during work hours. Everything else waits for designated check times. This stops the ADHD notification addiction while satisfying the autism need for structure."

Tool Stack Architecture:

- Task management that allows for both structure and flexibility

- Note-taking systems that accommodate non-linear thinking

- Time management tools that account for time blindness

- Communication tools that allow for asynchronous processing

Browser Environment:

- Ad blockers aren't just convenience - they're cognitive protection

- Password managers reduce decision fatigue

- Tab managers prevent the "47 tabs of death"

- Reading modes strip out distracting design elements

The Second Brain System: Many AuDHD people benefit from externalizing executive function into digital systems. This isn't weakness - it's augmentation. Your phone becomes your working memory, your calendar becomes your time perception, your notes become your retrieval system.

Social Architecture: Curating Your Support Network

Your social environment needs as much intentional design as your physical space. The wrong social configuration can drain you faster than any sensory assault.

Energy Vampires vs. Energy Generators: Some people drain your batteries; others charge them. This isn't about good or bad people - it's about neurological compatibility. That perfectly nice neurotypical colleague who needs lots of small talk might be exhausting. That "weird" neurodivergent friend who infodumps about trains might be energizing.

Track your energy after social interactions. You'll find patterns. Use these patterns to architect your social environment.

The Concentric Circles Model:

- Inner circle: People who get you without explanation

- Middle circle: People who try to understand and accept

- Outer circle: Necessary but draining interactions

- Outside the circles: People you don't need to engage with

Protect the inner circle fiercely. Limit middle circle access. Structure outer circle interactions. Eliminate unnecessary connections.

Communication Boundaries:

- Scheduled "office hours" for availability

- Different response times for different people

- Permission to not respond immediately (or at all)

- Scripts for common social situations

Alex restructured their social architecture: "I stopped trying to maintain thirty shallow friendships and focused on five deep ones. I scheduled regular interaction with my energy-generating people and buffered interactions with draining ones. My social exhaustion disappeared."

Checklist: The Environmental Audit

Time to audit your current environment and identify optimization opportunities.

Physical Space Audit: □ Lighting: Type, intensity, color temperature, adjustability □ Sound: Background noise, control options, escape routes □ Temperature: Current state, control level, comfort tools available □ Texture: Clothing, seating, surfaces you regularly touch □ Organization: Visual clutter level, system functionality □ Movement: Space to pace, stim, stretch □ Retreat space: Somewhere to recover when overwhelmed

Digital Environment Audit: □ Screen settings: Brightness, color, dark mode options □ Notification settings: What gets through when □ Tool functionality: Does each tool support your brain? □ Information architecture: Can you find things? □ Automation level: What could be automated that isn't? □ Distraction management: What pulls focus unnecessarily?

Social Environment Audit: □ Energy mapping: Who drains, who energizes? □ Boundary clarity: Do people know your limits? □ Communication preferences: Are they explicit? □ Support system: Who understands your neurotype? □ Professional relationships: Structured appropriately? □ Recovery time: Built in after social interaction?

Sensory Regulation Tools Available: □ Visual: Sunglasses, screens, lighting control □ Auditory: Headphones, earplugs, white noise □ Tactile: Fidgets, comfortable clothes, weighted items □ Movement: Space to move, permission to move □ Pressure: Weighted blankets, compression clothing □ Temperature: Layers, fans, heating options

For each unchecked box, identify one small step toward optimization. You don't need perfect environments - you need environments that work with your brain instead of against it.

Your Environmental Power

Your environmental needs aren't special accommodations - they're operating requirements. Just like a computer needs specific conditions to run optimally, your brain needs specific environmental parameters to function at its best. When you stop apologizing for these needs and start designing for them, everything changes. Your environment becomes an extension of your cognitive system, supporting rather than sabotaging your unique brain.

Chapter 11: The Spike and Recovery Model

Your energy doesn't work like other people's energy. While they have relatively stable reserves that deplete gradually throughout the day, you have spikes and crashes, floods and droughts, hyperdrive and complete shutdown. This isn't a flaw in your system - it's a different system entirely, one that can achieve incredible things when you understand how to work with it.

The problem is you've been trying to manage your energy using neurotypical models. That's like trying to run a sports car using a diesel truck manual. No wonder you're exhausted. No wonder nothing seems to work consistently. You need an entirely different approach to energy management.

Understanding Your Unique Energy Patterns

Your energy patterns are more complex than simple "high" and "low." You have multiple energy systems running simultaneously, and they don't always align.

Physical Energy: Your body's actual capacity for movement and action. This might spike with hyperactivity and crash with autistic burnout.

Cognitive Energy: Your brain's ability to process information. This can be massive during hyperfocus but completely depleted by sensory overload.

Social Energy: Your capacity for human interaction. Often limited and slow to recharge.

Executive Function Energy: Your ability to plan, initiate, and switch tasks. Usually your scarcest resource.

Creative Energy: Your ability to generate new ideas and connections. Often highest when other energies are low.

Emotional Regulation Energy: Your capacity to manage feelings and reactions. Depletes faster than neurotypicals realize.

These energies don't move together. You might have massive cognitive energy but zero executive function. Huge creative energy but no social energy. Understanding these separate systems is crucial.

Tom tracked his energy patterns for a month: "I discovered my cognitive energy peaks at 10 PM when my social energy is completely gone. My executive function is highest at 6 AM when my creative energy is dead. I was trying to force myself to do the wrong tasks at the wrong times."

Your energy also follows different patterns:

The Intensity Spike: Sudden, massive energy that must be used immediately or it dissipates. Often triggered by interest, novelty, or urgency.

The Slow Burn: Lower but sustained energy that can last for hours if protected from interruption.

The Cascade: Energy that builds on itself - success creating more energy creating more success.

The Cliff: Sudden, complete energy depletion with no warning signs neurotypicals would recognize.

The Intensity-Rest Cycle Optimization

Your energy doesn't follow a smooth curve - it spikes and crashes. Fighting this pattern exhausts you. Working with it makes you powerful.

The Spike and Recovery Model recognizes that you're designed for intense bursts followed by deep recovery. You're a sprinter, not a marathon runner. But society is structured for marathon runners, so you've been trying to maintain steady paces that your system can't sustain.

Here's how to optimize your cycles:

Ride the Spikes: When energy spikes, use it immediately. Don't try to "save it for later" - it doesn't work that way. Have a list of high-energy tasks ready to deploy when spikes hit.

Honor the Crashes: Recovery isn't laziness - it's restoration. Your intense spikes require equally intense recovery. Plan for it, protect it, don't apologize for it.

Create Bridges: Between spikes and crashes, you have bridge periods where you can do maintenance tasks. Not high-intensity work, not complete rest, but gentle productivity.

Stack Cycles: Align different energy cycles. If cognitive energy spikes when social energy is low, schedule solo deep work. If physical energy peaks when executive function is strong, tackle organizational tasks.

Jennifer restructured her entire work life around cycles: "I do creative work during morning spikes, administrative tasks during afternoon bridges, and research during evening cognitive peaks. I build in recovery periods after each spike. My productivity doubled, but more importantly, my burnout disappeared."

Matching Tasks to Energy States

The secret to AuDHD productivity isn't having more energy - it's matching tasks to the energy you have.

High Cognitive + High Executive Function:

- Complex problem-solving
- Strategic planning
- Learning new systems

- Writing or creating original content

High Cognitive + Low Executive Function:

- Research and information gathering
- Reading and absorbing information
- Hyperfocus sessions on existing projects
- Pattern recognition tasks

Low Cognitive + High Executive Function:

- Organizing and filing
- Routine tasks with clear steps
- Email and basic communication
- Physical organization

Low Cognitive + Low Executive Function:

- Gentle creative activities
- Listening to podcasts or audiobooks
- Light physical movement
- Restorative activities

High Physical + Low Mental:

- Exercise or movement
- Cleaning and organizing physical space
- Errands and physical tasks
- Walking meetings or thinking

High Creative + Low Structure:

- Brainstorming and ideation

- Artistic expression

- Free writing or sketching

- Problem-solving through play

The key is having tasks ready for each energy state. No energy state is wasted if you have appropriate tasks matched to it.

Building Sustainable High-Performance Routines

Sustainable high performance for AuDHD brains isn't about consistency - it's about reliability within inconsistency. You need routines that flex with your energy patterns rather than forcing your energy into rigid routines.

The Skeleton Schedule: Instead of fixed schedules, create skeleton structures with flexibility:

- Morning skeleton: Wake window (not fixed time), non-negotiable minimum (medication, water), flexible options based on energy

- Work skeleton: Blocks of time assigned to energy types, not specific tasks

- Evening skeleton: Wind-down window, recovery activities, sleep preparation

The Energy Menu: Create menus of activities for each energy state:

- Hyperfocus menu: Big projects ready to tackle

- Low executive function menu: Simple tasks with clear instructions

- Recovery menu: Restorative activities that actually restore

- Bridge menu: Maintenance tasks that keep life running

The Transition Rituals: Create rituals that help you shift between energy states:

- Spike initiation ritual: Music, movement, or environmental changes that trigger high energy

- Recovery ritual: Systematic wind-down that signals rest

- Task transition ritual: Clear the previous task before starting the next

The Surge Protocol: When unexpected energy surges hit, have a protocol:

1. Quickly assess the energy type

2. Check the appropriate task menu

3. Set a timer (surges don't last forever)

4. Dive in without overthinking

5. Plan recovery for after

Michael developed his high-performance routine: "I stopped trying to have the same routine every day. Instead, I have routines for different energy patterns. High energy day? I have a routine for that. Executive function crash? Different routine. The routines are consistent, but which one I use varies. This flexibility within structure is perfect for my AuDHD brain."

Tool: The Energy Mapping Journal

Track your energy patterns to understand your unique rhythms. This isn't about judging or fixing - it's about understanding and optimizing.

Daily Energy Tracking:

Morning Assessment (Rate 1-10):

- Physical energy

- Cognitive clarity

- Executive function

- Social capacity
- Creative flow
- Emotional regulation

Midday Check-In (Rate 1-10):

- Same categories
- Note any significant shifts
- Identify what triggered changes

Evening Review (Rate 1-10):

- Same categories
- What depleted energy?
- What restored energy?
- What patterns do you notice?

Weekly Pattern Analysis:

- When do different energies peak?
- What combinations occur together?
- What triggers spikes?
- What causes crashes?
- How long do different states last?

Environmental Factors:

- Sleep quality and duration
- Nutrition and hydration
- Sensory environment
- Social interactions

- Physical movement

- Special interest engagement

Task Success Mapping:

- Which tasks succeeded in which energy states?

- Where did mismatches occur?

- What would you do differently?

Recovery Effectiveness:

- What restoration activities actually restore?

- How long does recovery take after different activities?

- What helps transition between states?

After a month, you'll see clear patterns. Use these patterns to:

- Schedule important tasks during reliable energy windows

- Prepare for predictable crashes

- Build in recovery before you need it

- Create realistic expectations

- Communicate your needs to others

Your Energy Mastery

Your spike and recovery pattern isn't a limitation - it's your power source. When you stop trying to maintain neurotypical steadiness and start working with your natural rhythms, you access levels of productivity and creativity that steady-state energy could never achieve. Your spikes let you accomplish in hours what others need days for. Your recovery periods aren't weakness - they're the price of that intensity, and they're worth paying.

The world needs people who can spike into hyperfocus and create breakthroughs. Who can see patterns during creative surges that steady minds miss. Who can produce bursts of innovation between necessary recoveries. That's you. Your energy pattern is designed for exceptional output, not steady mediocrity. Own it, optimize it, and watch what becomes possible.

Chapter 12: The Integration Challenge

When Traits Collide

Sometimes your brain feels like it's at war with itself. Your autism craves routine while your ADHD rebels against it. Your need for completeness battles your inability to sustain attention. Your desire for order conflicts with your impulse toward chaos. These internal contradictions can feel like being pulled apart, but what if they're actually the source of your power?

The integration challenge isn't about choosing sides or finding balance. It's about creating systems that honor both aspects of your neurotype, even when they seem completely opposed. Especially when they seem completely opposed. Because in that tension between opposites lies your unique ability to hold paradox, create novel solutions, and think in ways that single-neurotype brains simply can't.

Managing Internal Contradictions Productively

The first step is recognizing that these contradictions aren't flaws to be fixed - they're design features to be utilized. Your brain is built to hold opposing truths simultaneously. This creates tension, yes, but also incredible creative potential.

The Routine Paradox: You need routine (autism) but you also need novelty (ADHD). The solution isn't choosing one or the other - it's creating *novel routines* or *structured flexibility*.

Rachel solved this by creating what she calls "routine themes": "Mondays are always for deep work, but what project changes. My morning routine has the same skeleton but different flesh each day. I have structure and novelty simultaneously."

The Social Paradox: You crave connection (human need) but social interaction exhausts you (autism) while isolation makes you restless (ADHD). Instead of forcing yourself into neurotypical social patterns, create your own.

"I do parallel play socializing," explains Marcus. "I'm with people but we're all doing our own things. I get social presence without social performance. My ADHD gets stimulation, my autism isn't overwhelmed."

The Focus Paradox: You need to hyperfocus to feel satisfied (autism) but you also need variety to stay engaged (ADHD). This isn't contradiction - it's sophistication.

The solution is *serial monogamy with projects*. Intense, complete focus on one thing... then permission to move on completely. Not abandoning things half-finished, but completing intense sprints then switching entirely.

The Information Paradox: You need all the information (autism) but too much information overwhelms you (ADHD). You want to know everything but can't process everything.

This is where external systems become crucial. Your brain doesn't need to hold all the information - it needs to know where the information lives. Building a "second brain" in digital systems lets your autism know the information exists while your ADHD doesn't have to hold it all.

The Executive Function Workaround Toolkit

Executive function is where many of your traits collide most painfully. Your autism wants perfect execution; your ADHD can't maintain the attention needed for it. Your ADHD generates seventeen ideas; your autism gets paralyzed choosing between them. But there are workarounds.

The Initiation Bridge: Starting tasks can feel impossible when your autism needs perfect conditions but your ADHD is already bored.

Build bridges - tiny, specific first steps that require no decision-making.

Instead of "work on project," have "open document and write one sentence." Instead of "clean room," have "pick up five things." The specificity satisfies autism, the simplicity doesn't trigger ADHD avoidance.

The Transition Tunnel: Moving between tasks can cause system crashes. Create transition tunnels - ritualized ways of closing one task and opening another.

David uses a physical ritual: "I literally close my laptop, stand up, do three stretches, then sit back down for the next task. This physical punctuation helps both sides of my brain agree the previous task is done and the next can begin."

The Decision Matrix: When seventeen options paralyze you, you need external decision-making frameworks.

Create matrices for common decisions:

- If energy >7 and deadline <2 days: Do urgent task

- If energy <4 and social need >6: Gentle social activity

- If interest =10 and obligations =0: Hyperfocus permission

This removes the exhausting decision process while honoring both your need for structure and variety.

The Accountability Exoskeleton: External accountability can replace internal executive function. But it needs to be the right kind.

Body doubling (working alongside someone) satisfies both needs - the autism gets structure and predictability, the ADHD gets social stimulation and urgency. Virtual body doubling works too.

When Autism Says "Routine" but ADHD Says "Novelty"

This is the classic AuDHD challenge, but the solution is elegant: create routines that contain novelty, and novelty that follows patterns.

Rotating Routines: Instead of one routine, have several that rotate:

- Monday/Wednesday/Friday routine
- Tuesday/Thursday routine
- Weekend routine
- High energy routine
- Low energy routine

The meta-structure is predictable (autism happy) but the daily experience varies (ADHD happy).

Flexible Anchors: Keep certain parts of routine absolutely fixed (anchors) while others float:

- Fixed: Wake up, take medication, drink water
- Flexible: Exercise type, breakfast choice, work order
- Fixed: End of day shutdown ritual
- Flexible: Evening activity

Novel Systems: Create systems that generate novelty:

- Random task selector for equal-priority tasks
- Rotating workspace locations
- Theme weeks that change focus
- Surprise reward systems for completing routines

Kate found her solution: "I have a routine for having no routine. Every Sunday I plan the week, but I use dice rolls and random generators to add variety within structure. My autism knows what's possible, my ADHD gets surprised by what actually happens."

Creating Flexible Structures

The key to integration is flexible structure - systems rigid enough to provide support but adaptable enough to accommodate variability. Think of it as building with bamboo instead of steel - strong but flexible.

The Modular Day: Instead of fixed schedules, create modular blocks that can be arranged differently:

- Morning block (3 options based on energy)
- Work block A (deep focus options)
- Work block B (administrative options)
- Recovery block (restoration options)
- Evening block (personal options)

Each day, arrange the blocks based on your current state.

The Both/And Framework: Stop forcing either/or decisions. Create both/and solutions:

- Both structure and flexibility
- Both depth and breadth
- Both routine and novelty
- Both solitude and connection
- Both completion and exploration

This isn't compromise - it's synthesis. You're not meeting in the middle; you're transcending the dichotomy.

The Both/And Framework for Decision-Making

When your traits conflict, the Both/And Framework helps you make decisions that honor all parts of your neurotype.

Step 1: Identify the Conflict What does your autism want? What does your ADHD want? Be specific.

Step 2: Find the Underlying Needs Autism might want routine, but the need is predictability. ADHD might want novelty, but the need is stimulation.

Step 3: Generate Both/And Solutions How can you meet both underlying needs?

- Predictable stimulation
- Structured novelty
- Controlled chaos
- Organized flexibility

Step 4: Create Implementation Strategies Make it concrete and actionable.

Step 5: Build in Adjustment Mechanisms What will you do if it's not working? How will you know? How will you adjust?

Example: Choosing a career path

- Autism wants: Stability, expertise, predictable environment
- ADHD wants: Variety, new challenges, dynamic engagement
- Underlying needs: Security and growth
- Both/And solution: Stable role with project variety, or consulting in one expertise area, or teaching (stable) different courses (variety)
- Implementation: Look for companies with rotation programs, or build portfolio career, or find role with both routine and project work

Your Integrated Power

Your internal contradictions aren't bugs - they're features. They're what allow you to hold paradox, see multiple perspectives simultaneously, and create solutions that transcend traditional either/or thinking. Your brain is designed for integration, not despite the contradictions but because of them.

When you stop trying to resolve the tension between your traits and start using it as creative fuel, you become capable of innovations that neither autism nor ADHD alone could produce. You're not half-autistic and half-ADHD - you're fully both, and that integration is your superpower.

Chapter 13: Your Personal Operating System

You've been trying to run your life using an operating system designed for different hardware. No wonder everything feels so difficult. It's time to stop downloading neurotypical software updates and build your own operating system - one designed specifically for your AuDHD brain.

This isn't about coping strategies or workarounds. This is about architecting a complete life operating system that leverages your strengths, accommodates your challenges, and turns your differences into advantages. You're not patching bugs - you're writing entirely new code.

Conducting Your Comprehensive Strengths Audit

Before building your operating system, you need to know exactly what hardware you're working with. This isn't a generic strengths assessment - it's a detailed audit of your specific AuDHD capabilities.

Cognitive Strengths Inventory:

Pattern Recognition: What types of patterns do you see effortlessly?

- Visual patterns
- Social patterns
- System patterns
- Data patterns
- Narrative patterns
- Temporal patterns

Processing Specialties: Where does your processing excel?

- Deep analysis
- Rapid synthesis
- Cross-domain connection
- Detail detection
- Conceptual understanding
- Creative generation

Learning Superpowers: How do you learn best?

- Immersive deep dives
- Parallel processing multiple sources
- Hands-on experimentation
- System reverse-engineering
- Pattern extraction
- Teaching others

Memory Advantages: What sticks in your brain?

- Special interest information
- Pattern-based data
- Emotionally significant events
- System architectures
- Sensory memories
- Connected concepts

Behavioral Strengths Map:

Hyperfocus Domains: Where can you achieve flow states? *Innovation Patterns*: How do you generate novel solutions? *Social Contributions*: What unique value do you bring to groups? *Problem-*

Solving Styles: How do you approach challenges? *Creative Expressions*: How does creativity manifest for you?

Lisa's audit revealed surprises: "I always focused on my struggles, but the audit showed I have superhuman pattern recognition in behavioral systems. I can predict team dynamics with scary accuracy. That's not a weakness - that's a marketable skill."

Building Your Personalized AuDHD Operating Manual

Your operating manual isn't a fixing guide - it's a user guide for optimal performance. Think of it as documentation for your custom hardware.

Section 1: Startup Procedures

- Morning activation sequence
- Transition from sleep to wake
- Executive function boot-up protocol
- Energy assessment routine
- Daily intention setting process

Section 2: Core Processes

- How you process information
- How you make decisions
- How you solve problems
- How you learn new things
- How you create and innovate

Section 3: Resource Management

- Energy allocation strategies
- Attention direction methods

- Social battery conservation

- Executive function preservation

- Recovery and restoration protocols

Section 4: Interface Specifications

- Communication preferences and protocols

- Social interaction parameters

- Collaboration configurations

- Boundary definitions

- Support requirements

Section 5: Maintenance Requirements

- Daily maintenance tasks

- Weekly system resets

- Monthly optimization reviews

- Quarterly deep cleans

- Annual overhauls

Section 6: Error Handling

- Common crash scenarios and recovery procedures

- Overload protocols

- Burnout prevention and intervention

- Crisis management strategies

- Support activation procedures

Section 7: Optimization Guidelines

- Performance enhancement strategies

- Efficiency improvements

- Upgrade pathways

- Integration opportunities

- Growth directions

Your manual becomes a living document you can share with others who need to understand how you work, and more importantly, a reference for yourself when you forget your own operating instructions.

Creating Your Unique Value Proposition

Your AuDHD traits combine to create capabilities nobody else has. Your unique value proposition isn't despite your neurodiversity - it's because of it.

The Value Equation: Your systematic thinking (autism) + Your creative connections (ADHD) = Solutions others can't imagine

Your pattern recognition (autism) + Your rapid processing (ADHD) = Insights at unprecedented speed

Your deep focus (autism) + Your novelty seeking (ADHD) = Innovations that are both thorough and creative

Your detail perception (autism) + Your big picture thinking (ADHD) = Complete understanding at all scales

Articulating Your Value: "I solve complex problems by seeing patterns others miss and making connections others wouldn't consider."

"I create innovations that are both systematically sound and creatively breakthrough."

"I bring deep expertise combined with fresh perspectives."

"I deliver thorough analysis with creative solutions."

"I see both the forest and every individual tree, simultaneously."

Michael refined his value proposition: "I debug complex systems by hyperfocusing on details while simultaneously seeing systemic patterns. I find problems others miss and solutions others can't imagine. That's worth serious money in tech."

The 30-60-90 Day Activation Plan

Knowing your operating system is one thing. Implementing it is another. The activation plan makes it real.

Days 1-30: Foundation Building

- Document your current state
- Identify three keystone habits that support your OS
- Implement one environmental optimization
- Start energy tracking
- Begin building your operating manual
- Share your needs with one key person

Week 1: Observation and documentation Week 2: Small experiments with routines Week 3: Environmental adjustments Week 4: Initial manual creation

Days 31-60: System Implementation

- Establish your core routines (flexible structure)
- Optimize your primary workspace
- Implement task-energy matching
- Build your support network
- Create your communication templates
- Develop your transition rituals

Week 5-6: Routine establishment Week 7-8: Relationship restructuring

Days 61-90: Optimization and Expansion

- Refine what's working

- Eliminate what isn't

- Expand successful strategies

- Build redundancy into critical systems

- Create sustainability measures

- Plan next-level optimizations

Week 9-10: System refinement Week 11-12: Sustainability building Week 13: Future planning

Track progress weekly, adjust daily, celebrate small wins constantly.

Template: The AuDHD Advantage Blueprint

Part 1: Identity

- Core strengths (top 5)

- Unique abilities (AuDHD superpowers)

- Value proposition (one sentence)

- Mission statement (what you're here to do)

Part 2: Operations

- Daily operating rhythm

- Weekly structure

- Monthly maintenance

- Quarterly reviews

Part 3: Environment

- Physical space requirements
- Digital environment needs
- Social architecture
- Support systems

Part 4: Protocols

- Morning startup
- Task initiation
- Transition management
- Evening shutdown
- Crisis management

Part 5: Development

- Current growth edges
- Skill development priorities
- System improvements planned
- Support needs identified

Part 6: Integration

- How traits work together
- Both/and solutions in practice
- Paradox management strategies
- Synthesis opportunities

Use this blueprint as a living document. Review monthly, update quarterly, overhaul annually.

Your Activated Advantage

Your personal operating system isn't about becoming more neurotypical - it's about becoming more powerfully yourself. When you stop trying to run software incompatible with your hardware and start building systems designed for your unique configuration, everything changes. Tasks that were impossible become effortless. Challenges that seemed insurmountable become manageable. And capabilities you didn't know you had suddenly come online.

Chapter 14: Finding Your Tribe

Community and Collaboration

You've probably spent years feeling like an alien visiting Earth, trying to decode the strange customs of the neurotypical inhabitants. But here's the truth that changes everything: you're not alone. There are millions of us, and when we find each other, magic happens. Not the "inspiration porn" kind of magic - the real kind, where people finally understand your jokes, your struggles make sense to someone else, and your weird becomes our normal.

Finding your tribe isn't just about comfort (though that matters). It's about unlocking collaborative superpowers that emerge when AuDHD minds work together. It's about building support networks that actually support the way your brain works. It's about creating spaces where you don't have to mask, translate, or apologize for being yourself.

The Power of Neurodivergent Networks

When neurodivergent people connect, something extraordinary happens. The constant translation burden disappears. The exhausting performance of "normal" becomes unnecessary. And suddenly, you have energy for actual connection instead of social masking.

The Resonance Effect: When AuDHD people interact, there's often immediate recognition. Not diagnosis comparing, but energy recognition. The way someone jumps between topics, the intensity of their interests, the particular flavor of their humor - you know your people when you find them.

"The first time I attended an AuDHD support group," shares James, "I nearly cried. Everyone was interrupting each other with excited connections, info-dumping without apology, stimming without shame. It was the first time I'd been in a room where I didn't have to monitor myself."

The Communication Shortcut: With other neurodivergent folks, you can skip the neurotypical communication theater. Say what you mean. Share your whole thought. Jump straight to the interesting part. No one's offended by directness or overwhelmed by enthusiasm.

The Validation Ecosystem: In neurodivergent networks, your struggles are understood, not minimized. Executive dysfunction isn't laziness. Sensory overload isn't being dramatic. Hyperfocus isn't rudeness. Finally, you're not constantly defending your existence.

The Knowledge Exchange: Neurodivergent networks are information goldmines. Someone's already figured out the hack you need. Someone else has the perfect stim toy recommendation. Another person knows exactly which noise-canceling headphones work best. It's crowd-sourced life optimization.

Collaborative Advantages: Why AuDHD Teams Excel

Put a group of AuDHD minds together on a project, and watch innovation happen at warp speed. Not despite our differences, but because of them.

Parallel Processing Power: While neurotypical teams process sequentially (one person talks, others listen, repeat), AuDHD teams can parallel process. Multiple conversations, simultaneous research, branching explorations that somehow converge into brilliant solutions.

Hyperfocus Relay: When one person's hyperfocus wanes, another's kicks in. Projects get 24/7 attention without anyone burning out. It's like having a hyperfocus tag team.

Pattern Recognition Network: Each AuDHD brain recognizes different patterns. Together, you create a pattern recognition network that spots connections no individual could see. It's collective genius.

Creative Chaos Synergy: The ADHD chaos generation combined with autistic systematization, multiplied across team members, creates innovation engines. Ideas bounce and build, getting refined and expanded with each iteration.

Sarah's design team of all neurodivergent creators revolutionized their agency: "We work completely differently than neurotypical teams. We'll have three people researching simultaneously while two are designing and another is documenting patterns. It looks like chaos, but we produce innovative solutions at triple the rate of traditional teams."

Building Your Personal Board of Directors

You need different people for different support functions. Your personal board of directors isn't about hierarchy - it's about having the right support for every need.

The Translator: Someone who can help you decode neurotypical communications and situations. Often someone who's learned to mask well or a very understanding neurotypical.

The Anchor: Someone who grounds you when you're spiraling. They don't try to fix or minimize - they just provide steady presence.

The Catalyst: Someone whose energy amplifies yours. When you're together, both of you become more creative, more productive, more yourselves.

The Librarian: Someone who remembers everything - where you put things, what you committed to, what triggered that meltdown last time.

The Cheerleader: Someone who celebrates your wins, especially the ones neurotypicals don't understand. They get why organizing your pens by color gradient is actually a huge achievement.

The Reality Checker: Someone who lovingly tells you when your perception might be skewed by anxiety, burnout, or RSD (rejection sensitive dysphoria).

The Special Interest Buddy: Someone who shares at least one of your special interests and will happily info-dump with you for hours.

Build this board deliberately. These aren't just friends - they're strategic support partners who understand their role in your life.

Online and Offline Community Strategies

Building community requires different strategies for online and offline spaces, and you probably need both.

Online Community Building:

- Discord servers for specific interests or identities
- Twitter/X communities using AuDHD hashtags
- Reddit communities (r/AutisticWithADHD, r/neurodiversity)
- Facebook groups for local or interest-based connection
- Twitch streams where neurodivergent creators gather
- Virtual co-working spaces for body doubling

Online advantages: Control over stimulation, time to process before responding, easy exit if overwhelmed, finding niche communities, 24/7 availability.

Offline Community Building:

- Local neurodivergent meetups
- Special interest clubs
- Parallel play gatherings (crafting, gaming, reading)
- Movement-based groups (hiking, walking)
- Professional neurodivergent networks
- Sensory-friendly events

Offline advantages: Full bandwidth communication, energy exchange, shared physical space, immediate support, activity-based connection.

Kevin built both: "Online, I have my 3 AM crisis support crew and special interest info-dumping buddies. Offline, I have my Sunday gaming group and monthly neurodivergent professionals lunch. Different needs, different communities."

Resource Directory: Communities and Platforms

General AuDHD/Neurodivergent Spaces:

- AANE (Asperger/Autism Network)
- CHADD (Children and Adults with ADHD)
- Neurodiversity Network
- Actually Autistic Facebook groups
- ADHD Twitter community
- Wrong Planet forums
- 7 Cups (peer support)

Professional Networks:

- Neurodiversity in Business
- Autistic Women & Nonbinary Network
- ADHD Entrepreneurs Facebook group
- Neurodivergent Professionals LinkedIn groups
- Tech industry neurodiversity groups

Special Interest Based:

- Discord servers for every interest imaginable
- Reddit communities for specific combinations

- Twitch communities around shared interests
- Local meetup groups

Support Focused:

- Autistic Self Advocacy Network (ASAN)
- Local autism/ADHD support groups
- Peer support networks
- Crisis text lines with neurodiversity training

Creative Communities:

- Neurodivergent artists collectives
- AuDHD writers groups
- Maker spaces with neurodivergent nights
- Online creative challenges with ND participation

The key is trying different communities until you find your resonance. Not every neurodivergent space will fit every neurodivergent person.

Your Connected Future

Your tribe is out there. They're info-dumping about their special interests right now. They're creating parallel play Discord servers. They're building businesses that work with their brains instead of against them. They're waiting to meet you, to recognize you, to welcome you home.

Finding your tribe isn't just about having people who understand you (though that's life-changing). It's about unlocking collaborative possibilities that don't exist in isolation. It's about building support networks that actually work for how your brain works. It's about creating futures where neurodivergent ways of being aren't just accommodated but celebrated and leveraged.

When you find your people, you find your power. Not the power to become neurotypical, but the power to become fully, authentically, unapologetically yourself - and discover that yourself is exactly who the world needs you to be.

Chapter 15: The Future is Neurodivergent

The world is changing in ways that make AuDHD minds not just valuable but essential. The challenges facing humanity - climate change, technological complexity, social justice, systemic failures - require exactly the kind of thinking your brain naturally does. Pattern recognition across massive datasets. System-level analysis. Inability to ignore injustice. Creative solutions that transcend traditional boundaries. The future doesn't just have room for neurodivergent minds - it needs them to survive.

This isn't inspiration propaganda. This is practical reality. The same traits that make traditional environments challenging for you make you perfectly suited for the emerging world. While neurotypical thinking got us into many current messes, neurodivergent thinking might be what gets us out.

Why the World Needs AuDHD Thinking Now More Than Ever

Look at the major challenges facing humanity. Every single one requires the kind of thinking your brain excels at.

Climate Crisis: Requires seeing systemic connections between seemingly unrelated things. Your pattern recognition sees how butterfly effects cascade through complex systems. Your inability to ignore uncomfortable truths means you can't pretend everything's fine. Your hyperfocus on solutions could breakthrough where incremental thinking fails.

Technological Complexity: As systems become more complex, neurotypical linear thinking breaks down. But your brain naturally handles multiple variables, parallel processes, and non-linear relationships. You debug reality the same way you debug code.

Social Justice: Your justice sensitivity isn't a burden - it's a societal necessity. You literally cannot ignore systemic unfairness. While others can compartmentalize injustice, your brain forces you to see it, feel it, and act on it.

Information Overload: While neurotypicals drown in information overflow, your pattern recognition can extract signal from noise. Your special interest deep dives prepare you for the kind of expertise needed in an exponentially complex world.

Innovation Demands: The low-hanging fruit of innovation is gone. Future breakthroughs require the kind of deep expertise plus creative connection that AuDHD minds naturally generate.

Dr. Temple Grandin puts it perfectly: "What would happen if the autism gene was eliminated from the gene pool? You would have a bunch of people standing around in a cave, chatting and socializing and not getting anything done."

Emerging Fields Perfect for AuDHD Minds

New fields are emerging that seem designed for how your brain works.

Complex Systems Analysis: From climate modeling to economic systems to social networks, understanding complex systems is the meta-skill of the future. Your brain is a complex systems analyzer.

AI Ethics and Alignment: Teaching machines to think requires understanding thinking at a systematic level. Your explicit processing and need for clear rules makes you perfect for defining ethical parameters for AI.

Bioinformatics: Massive pattern recognition across biological data. The field is literally about finding patterns in chaos - your specialty.

Neurodiversity Consulting: Organizations are realizing they need neurodivergent thinking. Who better to help them understand and integrate it than someone who lives it?

Immersive World Building: From video games to virtual reality to metaverse platforms, creating believable immersive worlds requires the kind of systematic yet creative thinking you excel at.

Regenerative Design: Creating systems that heal rather than harm requires seeing connections others miss. Your systems thinking plus justice sensitivity makes you perfect for designing better futures.

Data Journalism: Finding stories in data, seeing patterns that reveal truth, connecting disparate information sources - journalism is being revolutionized by people who think like you.

Innovation Archaeology: Understanding why innovations succeed or fail requires pattern recognition across domains and time. Your brain naturally does this archaeological work.

Advocacy Through Excellence

The most powerful advocacy isn't arguing for acceptance - it's being so excellent that your value becomes undeniable. This isn't masking or conforming. It's leveraging your authentic strengths so powerfully that the world has to acknowledge them.

Excellence on Your Terms:

- Define success by your metrics, not neurotypical ones
- Build systems that showcase your strengths
- Create outputs that only your brain could produce
- Solve problems others can't even see

Maria revolutionized her company's data analysis by building visualization systems that revealed patterns no one else saw: "I didn't advocate for neurodiversity through HR workshops. I advocated by saving the company millions through pattern recognition they couldn't access any other way. Now they're actively recruiting neurodivergent analysts."

Making Your Thinking Visible:

- Document your process, not just your results

- Show the connections others miss

- Explain your pattern recognition

- Demonstrate your unique value

Strategic Positioning:

- Place yourself where your differences are advantages

- Choose environments that need your specific abilities

- Build niches where you're not competing on neurotypical terms

- Create roles that didn't exist before

Creating Systemic Change Through Success

Individual success creates ripples that become waves of systemic change.

The Demonstration Effect: When you succeed authentically, you demonstrate what's possible. Other neurodivergent people see paths they didn't know existed. Neurotypicals see value they didn't know they were missing.

The Network Effect: Your success enables others' success. You hire neurodivergent team members. You create neurodivergent-friendly systems. You become a node in a network of change.

The Innovation Effect: The solutions you create, the problems you solve, the innovations you generate - they change what's possible for everyone. Your different thinking creates different futures.

The Normalization Effect: The more of us who succeed visibly and authentically, the more normal neurodivergence becomes. Not special or inspiring - just another valid way of being human.

Tom's startup story illustrates this: "I built my company around AuDHD productivity patterns - intense sprints, flexible schedules, parallel processing. We outperformed traditional companies so dramatically that competitors started copying our 'weird' methods. We didn't just succeed - we changed how our entire industry thinks about work."

Your Invitation to Lead the Revolution

This isn't about waiting for acceptance. It's about creating the future where your neurodivergence is an advantage. The revolution isn't coming - it's here, and you're invited to lead it.

Your Revolutionary Acts:

- Work authentically instead of masking
- Build systems that work for your brain
- Create value only you can create
- Connect with others building the same future
- Share your knowledge generously
- Refuse to apologize for your needs
- Celebrate your differences as strengths

Your Revolutionary Contributions:

- Solutions to problems others can't solve
- Innovations that transcend traditional thinking
- Justice that refuses to be ignored
- Connections that revolutionize understanding
- Systems that work for all brains
- Futures that include everyone

Your Revolutionary Future: You're not disordered. You're not less than. You're running different software, software designed for the future we're entering. A future that needs pattern recognizers and system thinkers and justice seekers and innovation generators. A future that needs people who can hold paradox, see connections, and refuse to accept broken systems.

The future is neurodivergent because the future requires neurodivergent thinking. The challenges are too complex for linear solutions. The systems are too interconnected for siloed thinking. The injustices are too entrenched for people who can ignore them.

Your Time Is Now

Stop waiting for the world to be ready for you. The world needs you now, exactly as you are. Your pattern recognition, your system thinking, your inability to accept "that's just how things are," your hyperfocus, your creative chaos, your authentic communication - these aren't just valuable. They're essential.

The revolution isn't about becoming neurotypical. It's about creating a world where neurodivergent thinking is recognized, valued, and leveraged. Where different isn't less than. Where the unique capabilities of AuDHD minds are seen as the superpowers they are.

You're not just part of this revolution. With your unique cognitive toolkit, your pattern recognition, your system-seeing abilities, and your innovation capacity, you're equipped to lead it. The future is neurodivergent. And that future starts now, with you, exactly as you are.

Welcome to the revolution. We've been waiting for you.

Appendix A: The AuDHD Advantage Toolkit

This toolkit isn't theoretical - it's your practical survival and thrival kit. These are the tools, templates, and strategies that actually work in the real world when your brain is doing that thing it does. Keep this handy. Print it, save it to your phone, stick it on your wall. This is your emergency kit, your quick reference, your "what do I do when my brain is braining" guide.

Quick Reference Guides

The Energy State Quick Check

When you can't figure out what's wrong or what to do, run through this:

Physical State Check:

- Hydration level? (When did you last drink water?)

- Food timing? (Blood sugar crash?)

- Movement needs? (Body needs to move or rest?)

- Sensory overload? (Too much input?)

- Temperature? (Too hot/cold affects everything)

Cognitive State Check:

- Information overload? (Too many tabs open in brain?)

- Decision fatigue? (Too many choices made today?)

- Context switching overload? (Too many transitions?)

- Hyperfocus hangover? (Coming down from intense focus?)

- Executive function crash? (Can't initiate/organize/prioritize?)

Emotional State Check:

- RSD triggered? (Rejection sensitivity activated?)
- Justice sensitivity activated? (Unfairness detector going off?)
- Social battery level? (Depleted from masking?)
- Burnout approaching? (Multiple systems failing?)
- Overwhelm building? (Everything too much?)

The Task Matching Guide

Current State → Best Task Type:

High Energy + High Focus → Complex projects, learning new skills, creative breakthroughs

High Energy + Low Focus → Physical organization, brainstorming, parallel processing multiple simple tasks

Low Energy + High Focus → Research, reading, detail work, special interest exploration

Low Energy + Low Focus → Routine tasks, gentle creativity, consumption not creation

Crisis Mode → Survival tasks only, maximum self-compassion, recovery priority

The Communication Emergency Card

When words aren't working, point to what you need:

- I need processing time
- I'm overwhelmed and need space
- I can't make decisions right now
- I need to move/stim

- Sensory overload - please reduce input
- I want to connect but can't talk
- I need help but don't know what kind
- Executive function isn't working
- I'll respond when I can
- I'm not upset with you, just overwhelmed

Downloadable Worksheets and Templates

The Daily Energy Tracker

Morning Rating (1-10):

- Physical: ___
- Cognitive: ___
- Social: ___
- Executive Function: ___
- Creative: ___
- Sensory Tolerance: ___

Afternoon Check-in: (Same categories)

Evening Review: (Same categories)

What helped today: _____ What hurt today: _____ Tomorrow's priority based on today's pattern: _____

The Special Interest Career Mapper

Interest: _____ Time spent weekly: _____ Years of engagement: _____

Skills developed through this interest:

1. _____

2. _____

3. _____

Problems this knowledge could solve:

1. _____

2. _____

3. _____

People who need this expertise:

1. _____

2. _____

3. _____

Potential career applications:

1. _____

2. _____

3. _____

The Burnout Prevention Checklist

Daily Non-Negotiables: □ Medication taken □ Water consumed (track amount: ___) □ Protein eaten □ Movement of any kind □ One transition ritual completed □ Five minutes of special interest time □ Sensory regulation check

Weekly Maintenance: □ Full recharge day scheduled □ Social obligations reviewed and edited □ Environment optimization check □ Support system check-in □ Executive function systems updated □ Celebration of wins (even tiny ones)

The Crisis Management Protocol

When everything is falling apart:

1. **Immediate Stabilization**:
   - Safe space secured
   - Sensory input minimized
   - Breathing (box breathing: 4-4-4-4)
   - Water sip
   - Trusted person notified if needed

2. **Basic Needs**:
   - Medication check
   - Food (even just crackers)
   - Comfortable clothes
   - Temperature adjustment
   - Light adjustment

3. **Recovery Actions**:
   - Cancel non-essential commitments
   - Activate support system
   - Engage comfort media/activity
   - Gentle movement if possible
   - Sleep when able

4. **Post-Crisis Review** (when recovered):
   - What triggered it?
   - What helped?
   - What would help next time?

o What can be prevented?

Digital Tool Recommendations

Task Management for AuDHD Brains:

- Todoist: Color coding, natural language input, flexible organization

- Notion: Build your own system, infinite customization

- Obsidian: Connected notes for pattern-thinking brains

- Forest App: Gamified focus for ADHD, visual progress for autism

- Goblin Tools: AI-powered task breaking for executive dysfunction

Time Awareness Tools:

- Time Timer: Visual time representation

- Be Focused: Pomodoro with flexibility

- Toggl: Time tracking that shows patterns

- Clockify: See where time actually goes

- Due: Persistent reminders that won't let you forget

Sensory Regulation Apps:

- Brain.fm: Scientifically designed focus music

- Noisli: Customizable background sounds

- Tide: Combines focus timer with soundscapes

- myNoise: Advanced noise generators

- Portal: Spatial audio for focus

Communication Aids:

- Otter.ai: Transcribe conversations for processing later
- Grammarly: Reduce email anxiety
- Calendly: Eliminate scheduling back-and-forth
- Loom: Record video explanations when writing is hard
- Marco Polo: Async video conversations

Mental Health Support:

- Finch: Self-care bird that grows with you
- Sanvello: Mood tracking with patterns
- Youper: AI emotional health assistant
- Daylio: Micro-journaling for pattern recognition
- How We Feel: Emotion recognition and tracking

Emergency Strategies for Difficult Days

The "Can't Start" Emergency Protocol:

1. Pick the tiniest possible piece of the task
2. Set timer for 2 minutes
3. Do only that piece
4. Celebrate completion
5. If momentum builds, continue; if not, rest

The "Everything Is Wrong" Reset:

1. Change one sensory input (lights, sounds, temperature)
2. Drink water
3. Do five wall pushes or stretches
4. Look at something pleasant for 30 seconds

5. Pick one tiny thing to fix

The "People Are Too Much" Escape Plan:

- Pre-written text: "Experiencing overload, need to step away"
- Bathroom reset (quiet moment, cold water on wrists)
- Irish goodbye permission (just leave when needed)
- Scheduled "phone calls" as escape routes
- Designated recovery space identified in advance

The "Words Aren't Working" Communication Kit:

- Emoji-only responses accepted
- Voice memos instead of text
- Drawing or diagram communication
- Pre-written scripts for common situations
- Permission to communicate later

The "Executive Function Is Offline" Survival Mode:

- Eat anything, even if it's crackers for dinner
- Wear yesterday's clothes if they're clean enough
- Use paper plates to avoid dishes
- Order groceries for delivery
- Ask for help without shame

Your Toolkit, Your Rules

This toolkit isn't prescriptive - it's descriptive. Take what works, modify what needs adjusting, ignore what doesn't fit. Your brain is unique even within the AuDHD community, so your toolkit should be too. The point isn't to follow these perfectly but to have options when your usual strategies aren't available.

Build your own toolkit over time. Notice what works, document it, and add it to your personal collection. Share with others in the community - your solution might be exactly what someone else needs. We're all figuring this out together, one strategy at a time.

Appendix B: Resources and Further Reading

Knowledge is power, and for AuDHD brains, the right knowledge can be life-changing. This isn't just a reading list - it's a curated collection of resources that actually get it, that were created by and for neurodivergent minds, or that offer genuine insight rather than neurotypical assumptions about how we should work.

Books, Podcasts, and Research

Essential Books by Neurodivergent Authors:

Neurotribes by Steve Silberman - The book that changed how the world sees autism, showing our history and contributions

Differently Wired by Deborah Reber - Raising neurodivergent kids by a parent who gets it

ADHD 2.0 by Edward Hallowell and John Ratey - Updated understanding from psychiatrists who have ADHD themselves

Unmasking Autism by Devon Price - The reality of autistic masking and the cost of hiding who we are

The Autistic Brain by Temple Grandin - Thinking differences explained by someone who lives them

Divergent Mind by Jenara Nerenberg - Women and neurodiversity, including the intersection of traits

Podcasts That Actually Understand:

ADHD reWired - Eric Tivers (ADHD) coaches and interviews with practical strategies

Neurodivergent Moments - Real talk about the daily reality of being neurodivergent

AuDHD Flourishing - Specifically about the AuDHD experience

The Neurodiversity Podcast - Interviews with neurodivergent professionals and advocates

Ologies - Not specifically ND, but ADHD-friendly deep dives into special interests

Research Worth Reading (Available Open Access):

"Autistic peer-to-peer information transfer is highly effective" - Crompton et al. (2020) - Proves we communicate fine with each other

"Having all of your internal resources exhausted beyond measure" - Raymaker et al. (2020) - First academic definition of autistic burnout

"The double empathy problem" - Milton (2012) - Why communication breaks down between neurotypes

"Camouflaging in autism" - Hull et al. (2020) - The reality and cost of masking

Professional Resources

Career Development:

Neurodiversity Employment Resources:

- Specialisterne: Global organization getting autistic people into tech careers

- Neurodiversity @ Work Employer Roundtable: Companies actively recruiting ND talent

- Mentra: Job platform matching neurodivergent talent with inclusive employers

- Neurodiversity Career Coaching: Specialists who understand our challenges

Entrepreneurship Support:

- Entrepreneur First's Neurodivergent Founder Program
- ADHD Entrepreneur Facebook Groups
- Autistic Entrepreneurs Network
- Freelancing guides specifically for neurodivergent professionals

Education Resources:

College/University Support:

- AHEAD: Association on Higher Education and Disability
- College Autism Network
- ADHD Coaching for Students
- Online learning platforms with ND-friendly formats

Alternative Education Paths:

- Coding bootcamps with neurodivergent support
- Trade schools with sensory accommodations
- Online certifications with flexible pacing
- Mentorship programs in special interest areas

Legal and Advocacy Resources:

- Job Accommodation Network (JAN): Free, confidential guidance on workplace accommodations
- Disability Rights Education & Defense Fund
- Autistic Self Advocacy Network (ASAN): By autistics, for autistics
- CHADD Legal Resources: ADHD-specific rights and advocacy

Support Organizations

International Organizations:

Autism-Focused:

- Autistic Self Advocacy Network (ASAN): Actually autistic-led advocacy

- Autistic Women & Nonbinary Network (AWN): Intersectional support

- Asperger/Autism Network (AANE): Programs and support groups

- Wrong Planet: One of the oldest autistic online communities

ADHD-Focused:

- CHADD (Children and Adults with ADHD): Largest ADHD organization

- ADDA (Attention Deficit Disorder Association): Adult-focused support

- ADDitude Magazine: Practical strategies and community

AuDHD/General Neurodiversity:

- Neurodiversity Network: Cross-neurotype support

- The International Society for Neurodiversity: Professional organization

- Neurodivergent Liberation Coalition: Activism and community

Local Support Options:

Finding local support:

1. Search "[your city] neurodivergent support group"

2. Check Meetup.com for ND groups

3. Contact local disability services organizations

4. Ask at libraries - many host ND-friendly groups

5. Check with local colleges - often have groups open to community

Online Communities That Don't Suck:

- Actually Autistic Facebook groups (verify they're actually autistic-led)

- r/AutisticWithADHD subreddit

- Discord servers for specific interests + neurodiversity

- Twitch streams with neurodivergent creators and communities

- TikTok #ActuallyAutistic and #AuDHD communities (great for quick tips)

Career and Education Resources

Finding Your Path:

Assessment Tools:

- O*NET Interest Profiler: Free career interest assessment

- 16Personalities Career Explorer: Personality-based career matching

- MyPlan.com Values Assessment: Align career with values

- Special interest → Career mapping worksheets

Neurodivergent-Friendly Fields:

- Technology: Programming, cybersecurity, data analysis, QA testing

- Creative: Writing, design, music production, content creation

- Science: Research, lab work, field studies

- Specialized: Translation, editing, specialized consulting
- Entrepreneurship: Building around your special interests

Accommodation Strategies:

Workplace Accommodations That Actually Help:

- Written instructions for verbal requests
- Noise-canceling headphones permission
- Work from home options
- Flexible scheduling
- Regular breaks for movement
- Email instead of phone calls
- Advance notice of changes
- Clear, explicit expectations

Educational Accommodations:

- Extended time on tests
- Distraction-reduced testing environment
- Note-taking assistance or permission to record
- Advance access to lecture materials
- Alternative assignment formats
- Clear rubrics and expectations
- Permission to step out when overwhelmed

Building Your Career:

Portfolio Building:

- GitHub for coders

- Behance for designers
- Medium for writers
- YouTube for content creators
- Personal websites showing special interest expertise

Networking for People Who Hate Networking:

- Online communities in your interest area
- Parallel networking (doing activities together)
- One-on-one coffee meetings instead of events
- Contributing to online discussions
- Building reputation through work, not small talk

Your Resource Evolution

Resources that help you today might not tomorrow. Your needs will change as you understand yourself better, as you build supports, as you find your people. Keep exploring, keep learning, keep finding what works for you. And when you find something amazing, share it with the community. We're all resource librarians for each other.

Appendix C: For Allies and Supporters

If you're reading this, someone you care about has AuDHD, or you're trying to understand how to create more inclusive spaces. First, thank you. The fact that you're here, trying to understand, means everything. This appendix is your guide to supporting without suffocating, helping without infantilizing, and creating environments where AuDHD people can thrive.

Understanding the AuDHD Experience

The first thing to understand is that AuDHD isn't autism plus ADHD like 1+1=2. It's more like mixing yellow and blue to get green - something entirely new emerges. Your person isn't "a little autistic and a little ADHD." They're fully both, simultaneously, all the time.

What It Actually Feels Like:

Your AuDHD person lives in a world that's simultaneously too much and not enough. They need stimulation but get overwhelmed. They crave routine but need novelty. They want connection but social interaction exhausts them. It's not indecisiveness - it's competing neurological needs.

Think of it like this: Their brain has two operating systems running simultaneously. Sometimes they work together beautifully, creating capabilities you can't imagine. Sometimes they conflict, creating internal struggles you can't see. They're not being difficult - they're managing complexity you're not aware of.

Daily Challenges That Aren't Visible:

Sensory Processing: The fluorescent lights you don't notice might feel like strobes to them. The background music you enjoy might make thinking impossible. That soft sweater might feel like sandpaper. They're not being dramatic - their nervous system literally processes stimuli differently.

Executive Function: They might be brilliant but unable to start simple tasks. They can solve complex problems but forget to eat. They can hyperfocus for 12 hours but can't switch tasks when needed. This isn't laziness or lack of caring - it's neurological.

Social Navigation: They're simultaneously analyzing every word, tone, and gesture while trying to perform the right responses while processing sensory input while managing their energy. Social interaction for them is like you trying to do calculus while running a marathon in a disco.

Time Perception: They might genuinely not know if something happened yesterday or last month. They can lose three hours in what feels like minutes. They're not being careless with time - their brain doesn't track it the same way.

How to Support Without Enabling

There's a crucial difference between supporting someone's genuine needs and enabling avoidance. The key is understanding which is which.

Support looks like:

- Respecting their need for routine while encouraging gentle growth

- Providing structure they can lean on without becoming dependent

- Helping them identify patterns and solutions

- Being a sounding board for their own problem-solving

- Offering accommodations that increase independence

Enabling looks like:

- Doing everything for them to avoid any discomfort
- Never challenging them to try new strategies
- Making excuses instead of finding solutions
- Protecting them from all consequences
- Assuming they can't rather than asking how they could

Practical Support Strategies:

Be the External Executive Function (temporarily): Help them break down tasks, but teach the process. "Let's figure out the first step together" rather than "I'll handle this for you."

Body Doubling: Just being present while they work can help. You don't need to help - just exist in the same space. It's magical for ADHD brains.

Transition Assistance: Give warnings before changes. "In 15 minutes, we need to leave." Then "10 minutes." Then "5 minutes." It helps their brain prepare for the shift.

Sensory Advocacy: Help create sensory-friendly environments. Ask "What would make this space more comfortable for you?" Then actually make those changes.

Pattern Recognition: Help them see their own patterns. "I've noticed you work best when..." This builds self-awareness without judgment.

Creating Inclusive Environments

Inclusion isn't about special treatment - it's about removing unnecessary barriers. Small changes can make spaces accessible for AuDHD people without negatively impacting anyone else.

Physical Space Adaptations:

Lighting:

- Offer lamp lighting instead of only overheads

- Allow sunglasses indoors if needed
- Provide spaces with natural light
- Dim harsh fluorescents when possible

Sound:

- Create quiet zones
- Allow noise-canceling headphones
- Offer written alternatives to verbal instructions
- Keep background music optional, not mandatory

Movement:

- Standing desk options
- Permission to pace or fidget
- Walking meetings
- Flexible seating arrangements

Social Environment Adaptations:

Meeting Culture:

- Agendas sent in advance
- Clear objectives and outcomes
- Written summaries of decisions
- Options to contribute via text/email

Communication Norms:

- Normalize direct communication
- Make subtext explicit
- Allow processing time

- Welcome clarifying questions

Social Events:

- Quiet spaces for retreat
- Structured activities option
- Clear start and end times
- Permission to leave early

Policy Adaptations:

- Flexible work hours
- Work from home options
- Clear, written expectations
- Regular feedback, not annual surprises
- Focus on outcomes, not appearance of productivity

Communication Tips for Neurotypicals

Communicating across neurotypes requires intention and adjustment from both sides. Here's how to bridge the gap from your end.

Be Explicit and Direct: Say what you mean. Don't hint. Don't assume they'll pick up subtext. "I need you to finish the report by Friday" not "It would be nice if the report was done soon."

Avoid Idioms and Metaphors (or explain them): "Let's touch base" might be confusing. "Let's have a brief meeting to update each other" is clear.

Give Processing Time: After asking a question or giving information, pause. They might need time to process. Silence doesn't mean they didn't hear you.

Use Multiple Communication Channels: Follow verbal conversations with written summaries. Provide information in multiple formats. Some people process better reading, others listening.

Respect Stimming: If they're fidgeting, rocking, or using repetitive movements, that's helping them think and regulate. Don't ask them to stop unless it's genuinely disruptive.

Believe Them: When they say the lights are too bright, the tag is unbearable, or they need to leave, believe them. They're not exaggerating.

Learn Their Communication Style:

- Do they prefer text or calls?

- Do they need advance notice of conversations?

- Are they better in morning or evening?

- What's their optimal interaction length?

Common Misunderstandings to Avoid:

"You don't look autistic/ADHD" - There's no look. This invalidates their experience.

"Everyone's a little ADHD/autistic" - No, they're not. This minimizes real neurological differences.

"You just need to try harder" - They're likely trying harder than you can imagine.

"You're using it as an excuse" - They're explaining, not excusing.

"You weren't like this before" - They were always like this; they were just masking.

Your Role as an Ally

Being an ally isn't about fixing or saving anyone. It's about:

- Learning and respecting differences

- Advocating for inclusion
- Challenging ableist assumptions
- Creating spaces where people can be authentic
- Amplifying neurodivergent voices
- Fighting for systemic change

Your AuDHD person doesn't need you to understand everything about their experience. They need you to believe their experience is real, respect their needs, and support their self-advocacy. They need you to see their differences not as deficits to be corrected but as variations to be accommodated and even celebrated.

The Partnership Approach

The best support comes from partnership. Ask what helps. Listen to the answer. Try it. Adjust based on feedback. Repeat. Your AuDHD person is the expert on their own brain. Your role is to be a collaborative partner in creating environments and relationships that work for both of you.

Being an ally is an ongoing process of learning, adjusting, and growing. You'll make mistakes. That's okay. What matters is that you're trying, you're open to feedback, and you're committed to creating a world where neurodivergent people don't have to choose between being themselves and being successful.

References

- **Armstrong, T.** (2010). *Neurodiversity: Discovering the extraordinary gifts of autism, ADHD, dyslexia, and other brain differences.* Da Capo Lifelong Books.

- **Ashburner, J., Ziviani, J., & Rodger, S.** (2008). Sensory processing and classroom emotional, behavioral, and educational outcomes in children with autism spectrum disorder. *American Journal of Occupational Therapy, 62*(5), 564–573.

- **Ashinoff, B. K., & Abu-Akel, A.** (2021). Hyperfocus: The forgotten frontier of attention. *Psychological Research, 85*(1), 1–19.

- **Attwood, T.** (2006). *The complete guide to Asperger's syndrome.* Jessica Kingsley Publishers.

- **Baron-Cohen, S.** (2009). Autism: The empathizing–systemizing (E-S) theory. *Annals of the New York Academy of Sciences, 1156*(1), 68–80.

- **Baron-Cohen, S., Wheelwright, S., Burtenshaw, A., & Hobson, E.** (2007). Mathematical talent is linked to autism. *Human Nature, 18*(2), 125–131.

- **Belcher, H. L., Morein-Zamir, S., Mandy, W., & Ford, R. M.** (2022). Camouflaging intent, first impressions, and age of ASC diagnosis in autistic men and women. *Journal of Autism and Developmental Disorders, 52*(8), 3413–3426.

- **Bora, E., & Pantelis, C.** (2015). Meta-analysis of cognitive impairment in first-episode bipolar disorder: Comparison with first-episode schizophrenia and healthy controls. *Schizophrenia Bulletin, 41*(5), 1095–1104.

- **Brown, T. E.** (2013). *A new understanding of ADHD in children and adults: Executive function impairments.* Routledge.

- **Cage, E., & Troxell-Whitman, Z.** (2019). Understanding the reasons, contexts and costs of camouflaging for autistic adults. *Journal of Autism and Developmental Disorders, 49*(5), 1899–1911.

- **Carver, C. S., & White, T. L.** (1994). Behavioral inhibition, behavioral activation, and affective responses to impending reward and punishment. *Journal of Personality and Social Psychology, 67*(2), 319–333.

- **Chrysikou, E. G.** (2019). Creativity in and out of (cognitive) control. *Current Opinion in Behavioral Sciences, 27*, 94–99.

- **Craig, F., Margari, F., Legrottaglie, A. R., Palumbi, R., De Giambattista, C., & Margari, L.** (2016). A review of executive function deficits in autism spectrum disorder and attention-deficit/hyperactivity disorder. *Neuropsychiatric Disease and Treatment, 12*, 1191–1202.

- **Crompton, C. J., Hallett, S., Ropar, D., Flynn, E., & Fletcher-Watson, S.** (2020). "I never realized everybody felt as happy as I do when I am around autistic people": A thematic analysis of autistic adults' relationships with autistic and neurotypical friends and family. *Autism, 24*(6), 1438–1448.

- **Crompton, C. J., Ropar, D., Evans-Williams, C. V., Flynn, E. G., & Fletcher-Watson, S.** (2020). Autistic peer-to-peer information transfer is highly effective. *Autism, 24*(7), 1704–1712.

- **Esterman, M., & Rothlein, D.** (2019). Models of sustained attention. *Current Opinion in Psychology, 29*, 174–180.

- **Fletcher-Watson, S., Adams, J., Brook, K., Charman, T., Crane, L., Cusack, J., Leekam, S., Milton, D., Parr, J., & Pellicano, E.** (2019). Making the future together: Shaping autism research through meaningful participation. *Autism, 23*(4), 943–953.

- **Grandin, T.** (2006). *Thinking in pictures: My life with autism*. Vintage.

- **Grandin, T., & Panek, R.** (2013). *The autistic brain: Thinking across the spectrum*. Houghton Mifflin Harcourt.

- **Grove, R., Hoekstra, R. A., Wierda, M., & Begeer, S.** (2018). Special interests and subjective wellbeing in autistic adults. *Autism Research, 11*(5), 766–775.

- **Happé, F., & Frith, U.** (2006). The weak coherence account: Detail-focused cognitive style in autism spectrum disorders. *Journal of Autism and Developmental Disorders, 36*(1), 5–25.

- **Happé, F., & Vital, P.** (2009). What aspects of autism predispose to talent? *Philosophical Transactions of the Royal Society B, 364*(1522), 1369–1375.

- **Hendrickx, S.** (2010). *The adolescent and adult neuro-diversity handbook: Asperger's syndrome, ADHD, dyslexia, dyspraxia, and related conditions*. Jessica Kingsley Publishers.

- **Howe, F. E. J., & Stagg, S. D.** (2016). How sensory experiences affect adolescents with an autistic spectrum condition within the classroom. *Journal of Autism and Developmental Disorders, 46*(5), 1656–1668.

- **Hull, L., Petrides, K. V., & Mandy, W.** (2020). The female autism phenotype and camouflaging: A narrative review. *Review Journal of Autism and Developmental Disorders, 7*(4), 306–317.

- **Jordan, C. J., & Caldwell-Harris, C. L.** (2012). Understanding differences in neurotypical and autism spectrum special interests through internet forums. *Intellectual and Developmental Disabilities, 50*(5), 391–402.

- **Kasirer, A., & Mashal, N.** (2014). Verbal creativity in autism: Comprehension and generation of metaphoric language in high-functioning autism spectrum disorder and typical development. *Frontiers in Human Neuroscience, 8*, 615.

- **Lai, M.-C., Kassee, C., Besney, R., Bonato, S., Hull, L., Mandy, W., Szatmari, P., & Ameis, S. H.** (2019). Prevalence of co-occurring mental health diagnoses in the autism population: A systematic review and meta-analysis. *The Lancet Psychiatry, 6*(10), 819–829.

- **Mantzalas, J., Richdale, A. L., & Dissanayake, C.** (2022). A conceptual model of risk and protective factors for autistic burnout. *Autism Research, 15*(6), 976–987.

- **Meilleur, A. A. S., Jelenic, P., & Mottron, L.** (2015). Prevalence of clinically and empirically defined talents and strengths in autism. *Journal of Autism and Developmental Disorders, 45*(5), 1354–1367.

- **Milton, D. E.** (2012). On the ontological status of autism: The "double empathy problem". *Disability & Society, 27*(6), 883–887.

- **Morrison, K. E., DeBrabander, K. M., Faso, D. J., & Sasson, N. J.** (2019). Variability in first impressions of autistic adults made by neurotypical raters is driven more by characteristics of the rater than by characteristics of autistic adults. *Autism, 23*(7), 1817–1829.

- **Mottron, L., Dawson, M., Soulières, I., Hubert, B., & Burack, J.** (2006). Enhanced perceptual functioning in autism: An update, and eight principles of autistic perception. *Journal of Autism and Developmental Disorders, 36*(1), 27–43.

- **Nijstad, B. A., De Dreu, C. K., Rietzschel, E. F., & Baas, M.** (2010). The dual pathway to creativity model: Creative ideation as a function of flexibility and persistence. *European Review of Social Psychology, 21*(1), 34–77.

- **Pellicano, E., Dinsmore, A., & Charman, T.** (2014). What should autism research focus upon? Community views and priorities from the United Kingdom. *Autism, 18*(7), 756–770.

- **Raymaker, D. M., Teo, A. R., Steckler, N. A., Lentz, B., Scharer, M., Delos Santos, A., & Nicolaidis, C.** (2020). "Having all of your internal resources exhausted beyond measure and being left with no clean-up crew": Defining autistic burnout. *Autism in Adulthood, 2*(2), 132–143.

- **Robertson, C. E., & Baron-Cohen, S.** (2017). Sensory perception in autism. *Nature Reviews Neuroscience, 18*(11), 671–684.

- **Robertson, S. M.** (2010). Neurodiversity, quality of life, and autistic adults: Shifting research and professional focuses onto real-life challenges. *Disability Studies Quarterly, 30*(1).

- **Rong, Y., Yang, C. J., Jin, Y., & Wang, Y.** (2021). Prevalence of attention-deficit/hyperactivity disorder in individuals with autism spectrum disorder: A meta-analysis. *Research in Autism Spectrum Disorders, 83*, 101759.

- **Ritter, S. M., & Mostert, N.** (2017). Enhancement of creative thinking skills using a cognitive-based creativity training. *Journal of Cognitive Enhancement, 1*(3), 243–253.

- **Ruzich, E., Allison, C., Smith, P., Watson, P., Auyeung, B., Ring, H., & Baron-Cohen, S.** (2015). Measuring autistic traits in the general population: A systematic review of the Autism-Spectrum Quotient (AQ) in a nonclinical population sample of 6,900 typical adult males and females. *Molecular Autism, 6*, 2.

- **Saggar, M., Quintin, E. M., Bott, N. T., Kienitz, E., Chien, Y.-H., Hong, D. W., & Reiss, A. L.** (2017). Changes in brain activation associated with spontaneous improvisation and figural creativity after design-thinking-based training: A longitudinal fMRI study. *Cerebral Cortex, 27*(7), 3542–3552.

- **Sasson, N. J., Faso, D. J., Nugent, J., Lovell, S., Kennedy, D. P., & Grossman, R. B.** (2017). Neurotypical peers are less willing to interact with those with autism based on thin slice judgments. *Scientific Reports, 7*, 40700.

- **Silberman, S.** (2015). *NeuroTribes: The legacy of autism and the future of neurodiversity*. Avery.

- **Singer, J.** (2017). *NeuroDiversity: The birth of an idea*. Judy Singer.

- **Sowden, P. T., Pringle, A., & Gabora, L.** (2015). The shifting sands of creative thinking: Connections to dual-process theory. *Thinking & Reasoning, 21*(1), 40–60.

- **Stevenson, J. L., & Hart, K. R.** (2017). Psychometric properties of the Autism-Spectrum Quotient for assessing low and high levels of autistic traits in college students.

Journal of Autism and Developmental Disorders, 47(6), 1838–1853.

- **Vogel, S., & Schwabe, L.** (2016). Learning and memory under stress: Implications for the classroom. *npj Science of Learning, 1*, 16011.

- **White, H. A., & Shah, P.** (2011). Creative style and achievement in adults with attention-deficit/hyperactivity disorder. *Personality and Individual Differences, 50*(5), 673–677.

- **Young, S., Gray, K., & Bramham, J.** (2009). A phenomenological analysis of the experience of receiving a diagnosis of ADHD in adulthood: A partner's perspective. *Journal of Attention Disorders, 12*(4), 299–307.

- **Zabelina, D. L., & Robinson, M. D.** (2010). Creativity as flexible cognitive control. *Psychology of Aesthetics, Creativity, and the Arts, 4*(3), 136–143).

www.ingramcontent.com/pod-product-compliance
Lightning Source LLC
Chambersburg PA
CBHW071808090426
42737CB00012B/1998